Steal This Book

And Get Life
Without Parole

Bob Harris

D1737130

Common Courage Press   Monroe, ME

Library of Congress Cataloging-in Publication Data

Harris, Bob, 1963-
    Steal this book and get life without parole / Bob Harris.
        p.   cm.
    Includes index.
    ISBN 1-56751-171-6 (cloth). -- ISBN 1-56751-170-8 (paper)
    1. United States--Politics and government--1993- Humor. 2.
United States--Social conditions--1980- Humor. I. Title. II.
Title: Get life without parole.
E885.H37 1999
306'.0937--dc21   99-29380
                                                       CIP

Cartoons are by Tom Tomorrow. Used by permission.

Common Courage Press
PO Box 702
Monroe, ME 04951

207-525-0900; fax: 207-525-3068
orders-info@commoncouragepress.com

www.commoncouragepress.com

First Printing

Table of Contents

Part I

The Media
Don't Believe Everything You Hear, See, or Read

Part II

Sex, Race, Nationality
& Other Reasons to Hate Each Other

Part III

DC Comics

Part IV

$

Part V

Technology
Don't Sweat the Small Stuff,
the Big Stuff's Gonna Kill You Anyway

Part VI

Crime & Punishment

Acknowledgments, Praise, and Unseemly Genuflection

A number of creative people I like and respect from both the political and comedic worlds have given me encouragement which meant more to me than I think they know. In no particular order: Del Close, Steve Burrows, Jeff Cohen, Jim Naureckas, Michael Moore, Harvey Pekar, Joyce Brabner, Matt Groening, Paul Zimmerman, Pam Stone, William Blum, Mary Elizabeth Williams, Robert Scheer, Paul Krassner, and many others have been kind enough to convince me what I have to say is worth saying.

Which means if you don't like this book it's all their fault.

My personal appearances agent, G.G. Greg, and his two large and frightening dogs have been an enormous help over the years. I can only hope that paying him enough in commissions to build an entire wing onto his house will be sufficient to show my gratitude. If not, a couple sentences here probably won't cut it, but what the hell.

Andy Simmons at *National Lampoon* was the first guy to print any of my stuff in a national magazine. Lydia and Eric Sargent and Michael Albert at Z magazine were the first national publishers to pick up any of my political writing. Elizabeth Chamberlain of the *Cleveland Free Times* was the first person to ask me to write a regular column. This book would not exist without all these people's early encouragement.

My friends Susan Wolpert and Ray Lesser, publishers of the *Funny Times*, have tremendously good taste in humor, and I would write that even if they didn't print my stuff. Honest. Keith Hammond, Eric Umansky, Richard Reynolds, and Jay Harris at *Mother Jones* are also terrific to work with.

Norman Solomon introduced me to Common Courage Press when he asked me to contribute a chapter to his 1997 tome, *The Trouble With Dilbert*. I would have mentioned him in the above list of admired friends, but I'm mentioning him here instead, so I didn't.

Several of the chapter headings in this book were suggested by my very funny and unrelentingly Canadian friend John Wing, a comedian and poet who is comfortable holding court on topics ranging from obscure hockey players to folk songs of the Civil War. Whether everyone else in the room is comfortable is another question. Phil Proctor of the Firesign Theatre has also given me a number of suggestions, some of which are even related to my writing.

Special thanks are owed to Bob Sims at KNX radio in Los Angeles. Bob had enough faith in my work to give a plum commentator gig (one only held previously by Mort Sahl and Stan Freberg—so this was like getting Stephen Hawking's chair in physics) to a comic with no professional radio experience, a break I will always remember. And even when his political opinions were sometimes quite different from my own, he always had the integrity to let me spew onward. Dude is one of a kind. I am very lucky to know him.

Bob was also kind enough to introduce me to my radio syndicator, Dick Brescia, who I have never met face-to-face. However, he's really cool to hang with on the phone, I am already thankful for his support and advice, and he assures me that he does indeed exist.

Alex Trebek and the producers of *Jeopardy!* had absolutely nothing to do with this book, but there's a fair chance their show is where you first saw me, so if you actually buy this thing, I probably owe them thanks here. Everybody over there is really, really great, and I'm not just saying that because I'm angling to get back on the show as a contestant in Celebrity Jeopardy. Although that would sure as hell be cool. I'm coming after you, Al Roker.

"Tom Tomorrow," the crime-fighting cartoonist, was kind enough to let me pick out some of his funnier doodlings in exchange for not revealing his true identity as a suave millionaire playboy. Nor will I divulge his strange predilection for making his young male ward dress in a penguin suit. Mum's the word, "Tom."

On a personal level, far too many friends to mention have provided me with encouragement during my seemingly endless whining about this project. So many, in fact, that my next book will be nothing but a list of their names, along with broad hints regarding any damaging personal information I might reveal if they don't continue to encourage me.

However, three *very* dear people in particular stand out: Phil, you are the brother I would have asked for. Tara, I hope you stay my sister for a long time. And Michaeleh, I love you.

Finally, high praise and glory go to my publisher, Greg Bates, and the fine folks at Common Courage. Arthur Stamoulis did a neat job preparing the galleys and checking my, punctuation and spellinj. And everyone involved, from art to promotions, was remarkably good at their job. What this book gets right, they deserve much of the credit for. What this book gets wrong is entirely my fault. Except the part about Liddy Dole projecting all the sincerity and warmth of a greeter at Wal-Mart. Actually, the greeters at Wal-Mart are substantially kinder and more interested in others than that. I was just trying to cut her some slack. My apologies to Wal-Mart greeters everywhere.

Foreword

by Paul Krassner

This book reeks with irony, starting with the title, *Steal This Book*, which was stolen from Abbie Hoffman, and continuing with the subtitle, *And Get Life Without Parole*, certainly a punishment that blatantly doesn't fit the crime. And yet Bob Harris tries to pass himself off as a compassionate observer of our times. The nerve. The gall. The chutzpah.

Of course, there are folks who believe that Abbie Hoffman is a congresswoman from upstate and that I was a member of the Jefferson Airplane. Actually, Abbie was a radical activist in the '60s—he was a founder of the Yippies—and I am the editor of *The Realist*, a journal of social and political satire which I've been publishing for forty-one years (less an eleven-year hiatus when I temporarily ran out of taboos and money). However, I have managed to frolic with a few Paul Kantner groupies.

When *The Realist* first appeared in 1958, I was a lone voice. Now irreverence has become an industry. But it is irreverence for its own sake, point-of-view be damned. That's why it is such a pleasure, since I will be putting out only six more issues, to pass the torch to Bob Harris. He approaches current events with conscious innocence. He eagerly shares his awareness that not only is the emperor not wearing any clothes, but he also has an unabashed erection, pointing the way to further delusion.

While so many easy-listening stand-up comedians depend so heavily on generic joke references, angry name calling, and gratuitous profanity, Bob Harris relies totally on intelligence, wit, and insight. What fuckin' audacity! How dare he substitute original thinking to evoke laughter instead of relying on the automatic reaction of audience members who are actually applauding themselves for recognizing the references?

And so I'm happy to introduce you to a prolific writer who consistently combines facts and fantasy to expose the hypocrisy of one justifiable target after another, with the incisiveness of a humor surgeon. You may chortle, you may grimace, you may even weep, but one thing is certain, you will learn things never dreamed of by a focus group. But, as my father used to say, don't take my word for it, read the label. And enjoy your ass off.

The Ever-Expanding Worldview of an Angry Little Man

I write political humor.

Which is another way of saying that you've probably never heard of me before.

Most of my twenties were spent doing stand-up comedy in places named Yuk-Yuks and Snickerz and Uncle Funny's, sort of a decade-long Bataan Death March Of Fun.

I did a lot of topical material, always trying to play at the top of my intelligence. Which went over about as well as you'd expect in places named Yuk-Yuks and Snickerz and Uncle Funny's.

I was usually the middle act. I'd do my thirty minutes of carefully non-partisan jokes about Iran-Contra or whatever, setting the stage for the headliner—invariably a prop act, impressionist, hypnotist, juggler, contortionist, regurgitator, or on some nights all of the above.

Incidentally, I favor a constitutional amendment calling for the deportation of all prop acts to a remote tropical island where rich men can hunt them as game.

You've probably noticed that a lot of comedians have drinking and alcohol problems. Consider the lifestyle. you spend your whole life hanging around hotel rooms in unfamiliar cities, often without much to do, other than the waitstaff. The devil finds work for idle hands.

Unless his clubs are booked up. Then you call John Yoder or Tom Sobel.

Just kidding. John and Tom are comedy club bookers in the midwest whose rooms really aren't quite hell. Although Satan was easier to get on the phone.

My escape from all that was reading up on history and politics. I would read a lot of stuff, mostly famous mainstream dudes like William F. Buckley, George Will, and Dr. Suess, who I find makes up for a lack of topical analysis with really bright colors.

Eventually I stumbled across a magazine called *Extra!* published by a group in New York called Fairness and Accuracy In Reporting (FAIR). *Extra!* reported on news the networks didn't manage to squeeze in—and why they didn't.

This was fascinating. I always wondered about stuff like that. Turns out a lot of stories get killed because they might piss off the sponsors or they might embarrass the corporate ownership of the network or simply because they're not simple and visual enough.

There are lots of other reasons, too, and as I began to read more about who owns the media, I realized how much public relations and spin control have become the essence of almost every major facet of American life. So I started to study a lot more. I read a lot of Chomsky and Zinn. And I began to write humor where I knew exactly what it was that I wanted to say.

About eight years ago, on the second night of The Gulf War miniseries, which was a lot like *The Thorn Birds* only louder, I was the feature act at Catch A Rising Star in Cambridge, Massachusetts. The headliner was this nice lady named Pam who did musical impressions, including one of Cher lifting a little barbell with her tongue.

Catch A Rising Star was my very favorite club. It was right in the middle of Harvard Square, and you could count on playing to the smartest audiences in the world on a nightly basis. It's closed now. Instead it's one of those places where they sell books by the pound.

But back on this one night in 1991, Catch A Rising Star in Cambridge felt like the one place on Earth a political comedian would want to be. Outside, maybe a hundred students were tying up traffic and protesting the impending war with Iraq, as was also happening in dozens of cities across the country, although you wouldn't know it if you only watched the war on TV.

Inside, the room was pretty tense. And the opening act didn't help matters much by finishing his set with the following announcement (and this is my best paraphrase from memory):

"Thank you, thanks, everybody. We're gonna keep this show moving right along here now. But first, I should probably tell you I understand they have the war on the TV back by the bar, and apparently there's a report that Iraq has launched ballistic missiles toward Israel. We don't know if it's chemical or biological or whatever, but if you have, like, loved ones there, or you want to know what's happening or anything, we'll try to keep track of what's going on for you as the show goes on.

OK.

Your next act is a very funny gentleman who comes to us from New York City…"

And with that, I was introduced.

It was impossible to tell a joke that night without feeling like what Harry Chapin called the Dance Band On The Titanic.

So I didn't.

Instead, I just stopped my own act cold, talked with the audience about their feelings about the war, let them vent their fears, and got them to listen to each other for about twenty-five minutes. After which I did five minutes of dick jokes so Pam could come out and do the barbell thing with her tongue.

It was the best show I ever did. And I hadn't done a word of my act.

Which told me I needed to get out of stand-up comedy for a while.

Fortunately, colleges began inviting me to give humorous lectures on various political topics. And so since 1992, I've been to maybe 300 schools to talk about campaign finance reform, the history of the Civil Rights movement, U.S. government covert operations, and so on.

These are cool gigs.

About the same time, I started writing for Z magazine. In my stand-up days I had written for *National Lampoon*. But Z is even cooler since it:

a) carries lots of cool political articles by people like Barbara Ehrenreich and Ben Bagdikian and

b) is still just as funny as *National Lampoon*. Take that whichever way you prefer.

In the spring of 1996, the *Cleveland Free Times*, my hometown's free alternative newsweekly, asked me to write stuff like my monthly Z articles on a more regular basis. Other city weeklies soon began running the pieces as well. A couple of months later, I moved to Los Angeles, and the *L.A. Reader* picked up the column.

And they folded the very next week. Figures.

Hollywood, by the way, is *Lord Of The Flies* with better clothes.

I called the column The Scoop, which sounds really egotistical, I realize. But my intention was to draw a little muckraking illustration to go with it, a cartoon of a shovel digging through a bunch of smelly crap. Strangely, however, nobody wants to see a bucket of shit at the top of a column. Except for the people who syndicate Pat Buchanan, of course.

Anyway, fast-forward a little bit and suddenly my online column has subscribers in thirty countries. *Mother Jones* magazine reprints it on their website, and my daily rants are now broadcast by about seventy-five radio stations in the U.S. and replayed around the world by Armed Forces Radio. This all surprises the hell out of me.

Best of all, my Mom now hears me every morning on the little station in Ohio she listens to anyway, so as far as she's concerned, I'm now famous.

It's the same station Mom always had on when she was getting my sister and me ready for school. They used to play a lot of Porter Waggoner and Ernest Tubbs. Which I think explains why my serotonin levels are still so low.

And then in 1997 I went on the game show *Jeopardy!*

That's probably how you know me.

More on that in a minute.

Incidentally, you've read some of my work before. For example,

Keep Away From Fire Or Flame

was one of mine. I'm very proud of that one, although looking back, I don't think I've ever seen a flame that wasn't on fire, or vice versa.

May Cause Drowsiness

is also one of my better ones. I think it should be used a lot more, especially by any political talk show on CNN, Fox News, or MSNBC. Alan Dershowitz and Gloria Allred should have it permanently inscribed on their foreheads.

But my best work was probably

Not To Be Used As A Flotation Device

You'd be surprised how many things that applies to: toaster ovens, marble flooring, French Poodles—you name it. An amazingly small number of things in this world are really reliable flotation devices.

Anyway, that's how come there's this book in your hands and how I got to be the guy writing it.

I hope you enjoy reading it. Thanks.

Bob Harris, 1999

My Life in *Jeopardy!*

There's a good chance you only know my face from seeing me run through the game show *Jeopardy!* a while back. So here's what I wrote about it after the Tournament of Champions in 1998. This should answer your questions, so you can enjoy the rest of the book.

By the way, you're welcome to contact the producers and tell them you'd like to see me back on Celebrity Jeopardy, going head-to-head with like Tony Danza and Yasmine Bleeth. Now *that* would be some damn fine TV.

John Quincy Adams is going to kill me.

If you witnessed my $100,000 *Jeopardy!* Tournament Of Champions flame-out, you already know why. If not, let's back up.

My genetic Lotto ticket didn't reveal great strength, a square jaw, or even a full head of hair. The only good deal I've got going is the ability to remember vast amounts of useless crap. As I write this very sentence, I have no idea where my car keys are (honest), but I can recite the nine Greek muses in alphabetical order.

There's rarely much reward for that particular skill. At parties in college, I always lost the interest of attractive females to some larger predator, usually one whose job required his name to appear on his shirt. My only consolation was being able to describe the process really elegantly.

However, *Jeopardy!* hands out big chunks of cash in exchange for brain clutter. So a while back, I decided to take their contestant test.

I failed.

They give the test in the actual *Jeopardy!* studio to pretty much any warm body who calls and signs up. Usually, the warm bodies tend to be white, male, and upper-middle class. Not the show's fault; fact is, the producers are cool and strongly prefer a diverse group. But *Jeopardy!* requires education, and in the U.S., education requires money. So the line of auditioners often looks like a meeting at the Forbes For President headquarters.

The test consists of fifty tough $800 or $1000 questions, almost all concerning pop culture, the liberal arts, and other almanac stuff. The sciences are almost invisible. No big surprise; most of the writers, after all, *are* writers. So Rabelais might come up. Heisenberg quite certainly won't.

I'm at a disadvantage, since I don't read fiction—reality is plenty, thanks—and my major was electrical engineering. So I don't know squat about Antarctic Mythology and Cambodian Anagrams, but if the *Jeopardy!* buzzers stop working, just get me a soldering iron and stand back.

So I failed.

No shame. 120 people show up for a typical test. Maybe ten or fifteen get to stick around.

However, they do let you come back every six months if you're silly enough to keep trying.

So I failed again.

And again.

And again.

There are probably stalkers who give up more easily.

On the fifth trip, in February 1997, I resigned myself to endless washouts. Naturally, that was the day I passed.

After the test, you play a mock game against two other candidates. The key here isn't brains, but small motor skills. Many otherwise normal people have trouble pushing a button and speaking, as you know if you've ever been to a drive-thru.

Petty gamesmanship begins here. Auditioners begin racing on the buzzers, name-dropping alma maters, and kissing up to the producers, who are all really nice people but simply aren't there to find out that you like their hair.

Next comes a brief interview, no more complex than the question round of the Miss America pageant. You've already demonstrated intellectual and physical prowess. Now they're looking for interpersonal skills, to make sure you're free of major tics and generally Alex-safe. Twitching, handing out Constitutional literature, or stabbing a producer here are all good ways to stay off the show.

Finally, you have about five minutes to fill out a form asking you to list five funny and notable things about your life that can be summarized in two sentences. This is the hardest part, actually. Try it yourself. Most interesting things aren't that short, and vice versa.

I ran out of ideas and wrote down that I like squirrels.

After the interview, you go home and resume your life. They might call in six months. They might not call, ever.

I got a call from the producers in late August, inviting me to appear on the show in mid-September.

Some people think *Jeopardy!* gives contestants an outline of what to expect question-wise. Nope. In fact, since they can ask about anything in the history of human civilization, they flatly state that only a fool would actually try to study for the show.

I now had exactly three weeks to suck in a complete liberal arts education.

For twenty-one days, I went down to the library promptly at 9 a.m. and disappeared into the Reference section like Shoeless Joe into a cornfield.

By 7 p.m., I was home to watch the show, so I could study betting strategies, get a handle on probable categories, and evaluate my preparedness.

At 7:30, I went back to the books for review, keeping notes on my day's discoveries.

At no point did I ever work this hard getting my degree.

In retrospect, my need for revenge against all the single-browed name-wearing predators kicked in bigtime. Suddenly nothing else mattered. I blew off my girlfriend. Plates stacked up in the sink. Emails and phone calls backed up. Even my hygiene suffered.

In the second week, I started standing while playing along, instead of reclining on the couch, the better to acclimate to actual game conditions.

Three days later, I remembered that the video screens are far across the stage, so I moved my TV to the farthest corner of the apartment.

In the third week, I realized that stage lights would be in my eyes, so I rearranged my halogen lamps to cast a blinding glare on me from all directions.

About here is the point where my grip on reality appears to have weakened.

I also developed an ergonomically improved buzzer technique. See, you have to wait for Alex to finish the question and for an off-stage light to flash before you can answer, so most easy questions go to whoever has the best buzzer skills. After much experimentation, I abandoned the standard thumb-on-button technique, in favor of a desk-supported index-finger maneuver I consider the *Jeopardy!* equivalent of the Fosbury Flop.

Counseling would not have been out of the question.

And suddenly there I was, out walked Alex, and off we went.

Those first tapings now seem a complete blur. I clearly remember Alex asking me about squirrels, which I had totally forgotten ever having written. In fact, he teased me about admiring an animal that sneaks into backyards and steals food. To which I replied, "Well, maybe if *you* lived in a tree, you'd have to do the same thing." The audience laughed. Alex looked stunned, then amused. Apparently most contestants are too shy to tease him back.

I don't remember much else.

The games flew by. The other contestants hadn't prepared nearly as well. They had lives. I kicked ass.

At one point in the fourth show, I somehow ran the category of London City Guilds, about which—I assure you—I know *nothing*. But there I am on the videotape, asking "what are the Fishmongers?" with no hesitation whatsoever. I still have no idea how that happened.

I think my car keys are on the kitchen counter.

If you win five games, they give you a spot in the Tournament of Champions and about $40,000 worth of automobile. Which meant my last Final Jeopardy answer—one single question—was worth more money than the house I grew up in.

During the commercial, the make-up girl told me I looked pale. Yup. On the videotape, I look approximately as stressed-out as Nixon during the resignation speech.

After the shows aired, I was recognized everywhere for weeks. 20 million people really do watch. I couldn't eat a fast-food burrito without somebody asking me to repeat the $500 term for glowing bacteria on rotting meat (what is "bioluminescence?"). Which didn't exactly make the burrito any more appetizing.

Believe it or not, dozens of women began asking me out. I got marriage proposals from distant college professors and greeting cards from girls who broke up with me almost two decades ago. None of the women were under the age of 35, but at Lane Bryant, I was Elvis.

Lots of people ask what Alex is really like, so let me answer that once and for all: most people don't know this, but Mr. Trebek is actually a five-foot-tall black woman from Mississippi. They do wonders with make-up in Hollywood.

Look, Alex seems like a good guy and I liked him a lot. But it's not as if after the show we all strolled off to the lush *Jeopardy!* mansion to sit in a hot tub sipping Potent Potables with Merv and Henry Kissinger.

I will say that Alex has a pretty cool sense of humor. After the Great Squirrel Debate in the first game, I found I could both relax myself and distract my opponents by teasing Alex whenever possible. Everybody's pretty nervous their first time on that stage, and a lot of contestants are a little star-struck when Alex shows up and the game begins. Being the returning champ already gave me a psychological edge; appearing comfortable enough to gently *tease* Alex, as if we were old friends, increased that advantage visibly.

In any band of primates, proximity to the Alpha Male confers status.

And the guy responded well, good-naturedly dishing out in exchange. Whenever I made a stupid answer—about once a game—he often took a few extra seconds to ride me about it for laughs. I ribbed him a bit about his sheer damn suaveness and the perfection of his French accent.

Since I've already included my squirrel riposte, I'll give Alex the last word. One version of the promo spots for the Tournament of Champions included his final dig: "Some of the best minds we've ever had...except Bob."

OK, I admit it. I liked the guy a lot.

Which is also true of everyone else at the show. Fun as it is to dish, the truth is that I liked everybody. Of course, they *did* give me a lot of money, so that might color my opinion.

My fellow contestants were also bright and kind and wonderful to be around. Waiting in the green room is stressful enough that many of us bonded like victims of an airline disaster. Several have become close friends.

And if the regular season was hard on the heart, the Tournament was a complete flatline.

The Tournament was scheduled for January 1998, to air in February. Meaning that, after a brief visit with reality for a few weeks in October, I shortly returned to my routine of practice games played in blinding light with a distant TV.

Halloween came. I had forgotten to buy candy, so I handed out Gingko Biloba supplements.

Thanksgiving came. Instead of visiting my family in Ohio, I spent the weekend studying Famous American Indians.

On Christmas morning, I memorized Catholic Saints, and on New Year's Eve, I learned the names of 20th Century Dancers.

An intervention by the Cult Awareness Network might have been in order.

The Tournament contestants were the smartest people I've ever met: one guy completing med school at twenty-three, a seventeen-year old whizkid with 1600 SATs, and—most intimidating of all—a professor of Medieval Studies at Berkeley who had actually *read* all the books whose titles I had memorized.

If a nuclear holocaust had destroyed the world but somehow spared the *Jeopardy!* green room, these people could have rebuilt Western Civilization all by themselves. I would have done a lot of heavy lifting.

This was truly an ironic moment: for the first time in my life, in a roomful of people, *I* was the cute, stupid guy.

And—lucky me—the night before the Tournament began, I came down with a rampaging flu. Five minutes before showtime, I could barely stand.

This was my fault entirely. In exhausting myself for months, the one thing I had forgotten to study was Human Limitations.

If you saw that first match, you can no longer fear death, for you have already witnessed Hell. Against the smartest, quickest minds on Earth, I couldn't even remember that Snoopy was a Beagle.

The other contestants quietly snickered at my performance.

Fortunately, you also saw my desperation Hail Mary bet-it-all Final Jeopardy flail in which I pulled the city named for the Bishop of Hippo ("what is St. Augustine?") out of the nether regions of my anatomy, wobbling into the last wild-card slot as the gun sounded. My fever was peaking at 102. But somehow I had survived.

Destiny was on my side.

The next morning, my fever was down. I played the game of my life, racked up my highest score, and entered the two-day final as the first seed.

The Berkeley prof, Dan Melia, was the #2 seed.

Uh-oh.

The #3 seed was Kim Worth, a fellow stand-up comedian I had actually met once before, working a bar gig in a small town in Wisconsin that neither one of us remembers.

People of Wisconsin: you have a town up there so forgettable that two *Jeopardy!* champions can't remember a thing about it. You guys need a pumpkin festival or something.

As the final started in the afternoon, I was surprised to find I could still win on the buzzer, and I was ahead after the first round. But once Dan started nailing $1000 questions I could barely conceptualize, I realized he simply knew enough stuff that, at last, my buzzer practice wasn't going to make up for the holes in my database.

As Double Jeopardy ended, I knew my only chance to win was to pick a spot and try to nail a huge bet. I needed an edge. The broadcast date of this particular game was...um...February 12th. OK, that's...hmm...Lincoln's birthday. And, sure enough, the Final Jeopardy category was...*U.S. Statesmen.*

YES! We were probably about to get some obscure Lincoln question about the Union Party, Mary Surratt, or the Black Hawk War. If my hunch was right, I could close the whole deal before the second game even started. If not, I'd probably still wind up exactly where I was headed anyway. So I bet the ranch...

And the question had nothing to do with Lincoln. The correct answer to what they *did* ask was John Quincy Adams. And I probably would have remembered him if I hadn't been so flustered about Lincoln.

So this is what it's like to be the cute, stupid guy. It's not what it's cracked up to be.

Worse, now I had to spend another thirty minutes on national TV with no chance to win. So I played the whole thing for laughs, as did Kim. People like a good loser, and the audience roared appreciatively.

I can't speak for Kim, but I wasn't being gracious. I just don't know how else to look dignified while getting pasted.

My two-day total: one dollar. And a huge ovation.

Ah, what the heck. I'm not complaining.

At least I made an impression. I still get email from people who enjoyed the spectacle and want to say hi. Two major airlines have shown the Tournament finals as in-flight entertainment. And the Associated Press actually carried a national story concerning my buzzer technique (dubbed the "Harris Hit"), which I am told has since caught on with many contestants.

My agent thinks I should get ten percent of their winnings.

Sure, I still awaken sometimes in a cold sweat, haunted by visions of John Quincy Adams jumping at me from Lincoln's shadow. But y'know what? When I first began performing, I dreamed of making millions of people laugh, if just once in my life. And it finally happened, albeit in a really unexpected way.

It wasn't the prize I was playing for. But I'll take it.

P.S.—I know where my car keys are. They're in my blue jeans. I can hear them downstairs making a racket in the dryer.

Part I

The Media
Don't Believe Everything You Hear, See, or Read

Chapter One

The State of the Union
Unabridged

Highly-placed sources have leaked to me an early draft of Bill Clinton's 1999 State Of The Union Address. Phrases deleted from the final draft are indicated by *italics*.

Tonight, I have the honor of reporting to you on the State of the Union. *Tomorrow, everyone else in this room can go back to reporting on the state of* my *unions*.

Let me begin by saluting the new speaker of the House, *especially for not being the old speaker of the House*. Mr. Speaker, you asked us all to work together in the spirit of civility and bipartisanship. Let's do exactly that. *Please. For the love of God.*

Tonight I stand before you to report that America has created *what could be called* the longest peacetime economic expansion in our history, *if we weren't bombing Iraq or Sudan or sometimes even Pakistan and Bulgaria by accident on almost a daily basis.*

Thanks to the leadership of all of you, *and to a demographic drop in the number of eighteen- to twenty-four-year-old males who commit most violent crimes*, we have the lowest violent crime rate in a quarter century. *But really, Congress, you can take the credit anyway, if it'll get Henry Hyde off my keister.*

Thanks to Vice President Gore, we have a government for the information age, *in that it's completely locked at the moment and needs rebooting.*

America is working again. *Often two or three jobs at once.* But we cannot allow the hum of our prosperity to lull us into complacency. *I got lulled into complacency by a hum a while back, and just look at the mess that made.*

So with our budget surplus growing, our economy expanding, *and Hillary talking to me again*, now is the moment for this generation (*which is about to get old*) to meet our historic responsibility: to address the aging of America. *Just like our generation has been in favor of everything to our benefit for almost forty years.*

Without Social Security, half our nation's elderly would be forced into poverty. *Just like hundreds of thousands of kids were when I wiped out AFDC payments.*

I propose that we make the historic decision to invest the surplus in the private sector. *Unless this wildly overpriced market tanks,* this will earn a higher return, *and either way it'll goose the living crud out of Wall Street in the short run, and who the hell do you think I work for, anyway?*

But we must aim higher. We should eliminate the limits on what seniors on Social Security can earn. *After all, Wal-Mart always needs greeters.*

From its beginning, Americans have supplemented Social Security with private pensions and savings. Yet today, *thanks to the export of our manufacturing base, the dismantling of labor unions, and a minimum wage that isn't even close to enough*, millions of people retire with little to live on.

I propose a tax credit of $1,000 for the aged, ailing, or disabled and the families who care for them. *That'll cover maybe two days in the hospital. After which they should be just fine.*

Now there are children from more diverse backgrounds in our public schools than at any time in our history. *In spite of Pat Buchanan's best efforts.* We are well on our way to connecting every classroom and library to the Internet. *Whether the kids can actually read is another issue.*

Each year the national government invests more than $15 billion in our public schools. We must change the way we invest that—to support what works and to stop supporting what does not work. *As always, I am strongly in favor of good things and firmly opposed to bad things.*

No child should graduate from high school with a diploma he or she can't read. *Too many of them get elected to Congress.* Every school district should issue report cards on every school. *Although in some* areas, a simple body count will suffice. And all school districts must implement sensible discipline policies. *As long as we're wiring every classroom to the Internet, I propose we also wire every chair to the Power Grid.*

We also have to help the millions of parents who give their all every day. So let's raise the minimum wage by a dollar an hour over the next two years.

(Applause.)

As if any of us really thinks America's working poor will get all jazzed up about possibly making six dollars an hour in 2001

America's families deserve the world's best medical care. *Unfortunately, we can't all just move to Canada.* Managed care has transformed medicine in America. *Much the same way an eighty-foot drop transforms a cat.*

We must step up our efforts to treat and prevent mental illness. *If Bob Barr isn't a shining example, I don't know what you people need.* With sensitivity and passion, Tipper Gore is leading our efforts, *now that she's no longer hearing hidden Satanic messages.*

I recommend a national literacy campaign aimed at helping the millions of people who still read at less than a fifth-grade level. *Besides, we can't think of a better way to hurt Rush Limbaugh's ratings.*

Today much of the world is in recession, the most serious financial crisis in half a century. To meet it, the United States and other nations have strengthened the International Monetary Fund. *Which has thrown tens of billions of dollars—many of them yours—at Russia, Indonesia, and Brazil, all to no effect.*

We must help American manufacturers hit hard by the present crisis with loan guarantees and other incentives to increase American exports by nearly $2 billion. *Although a similar handout to American workers would have you all screaming "socialism" at the top of your lungs.*

And I ask the Congress again to give the president the trade authority to advance our prosperity in the 21st century. *I'm supposed to drag Chile into NAFTA before I'm outta here, dammit, now help me out.* And this year, we will conclude a treaty to ban abusive child labor everywhere. *Notice it's "abusive" child labor, not "all" child*

labor, which I'm sure my good friend and major fundraiser Phil Knight at Nike won't mind one bit.

We will defend our security wherever we are threatened and sometimes places we aren't, as we did this summer when we struck at Osama bin Laden's network of terror. Not that we hit anything in his camp or even knew for sure what we were bombing, and never mind that we pointlessly wiped out the only pharmaceutical plant in a country suffering a major famine. And America will continue to work for the day when Iraq has a government worthy of its people. So even though there's no democratic opposition in Iraq, I'm still ordering the CIA to throw almost $100 million of your money down another hole trying to support a coup.

You know, sports records are made, and sooner or later, they are broken. But Mark McGwire's a Republican, dammit, so the best suck-

up I can manage here is Sammy Sosa, a hero in two countries tonight.

(Applause.)

Forty-three years ago Rosa Parks sat down on a bus in Alabama and wouldn't get up, *no matter how many right-wing southerners told her to clear out. Come to think of it, I sort of know how she feels.* She's sitting with the First Lady tonight.

(Applause.)

This is a moment, as the First Lady has said, to honor the past and imagine the future. I'd like to take a minute to honor her for all she has done to serve our nation at home and abroad.

(Applause.)

I can't believe nobody ever complains about the way I absorb public affection intended for others the way the Chupacabra sucks the life force out of a goat. It's like an X-Files episode, but with better lighting. Geez, I'd introduce Mr. Hanky from South Park if I thought he'd get me an ovation.

We're now at the end of a century when generation after generation of Americans answered the call to greatness, overcoming Depression, bringing down barriers to racial prejudice, winning two world wars and the "long twilight struggle" of the Cold War. *And if Y2K hits, there's a fair chance we might get to do it all over again.*

A hundred years from tonight, another American president *or possibly a spokesperson for Microsoft* will stand in this place to report on the State of the Union. He—or she—*or it*—will look back on a 21st century shaped by the decisions we make now.

Let us lift our eyes, and from the mountaintop of this century, look ahead to the next one.

Century, not intern, I mean.

Thank you.

You may think you had a major choice in the 1996 Presidential election contest between Bob Dole and Bill Clinton.

Did you really?

Tell me: which candidate favored NAFTA? Who favored GATT? Both. Who favored maintaining China's Most Favored Nation trade status, in spite of continued human rights atrocities? Both. Who favored exporting cigarettes and lots of other fun stuff to Vietnam while tightening the embargo on Cuba? Both.

Who supported "right-to-work" laws, which drastically decrease the rights of workers to organize against poor working conditions? Both. Which candidate has claimed with a straight face that welfare cutbacks will ultimately help the poor? Both. Which one has claimed that the way to fight the drug war is to build more prisons? Which one advocates the extrajudicial seizure of assets and increased domestic surveillance? Both. Which one favored the death penalty? Which one favored expanding the death penalty to over sixty more crimes? Both.

Which one supported continued increases in Pentagon spending for high-tech weaponry, in spite of a rather remarkable lack of national enemies? Both. Which one continues to support weapons systems like the Stealth Bomber, the Osprey, and Star Wars (although nobody uses that name anymore), which simply can't work, and which the Pentagon isn't even sure they want? Both.

A lot of folks claim that there's a difference between the two when it comes to judiciary appointments. And there is: Clinton has so far nominated 187 people to the federal bench. Dole approved of only 184.

OK, let's get personal.

Which one comes from a rural midwestern state? Which one lays claim to sweaty small-town values, even though his entire adult life has been spent in government jobs in big cities? Which of the two has had business partners under investigation for Savings and Loan fraud? Which is advised by a staff of millionaire corporate attorneys? Which one is married to a highly assertive attorney from an Ivy-League school who began her career as a liberal crusader but later became a corporate sell-out, and later caused him embarrassment for her involvement in questionable real estate dealings?

Both again.

Sure, there were minor policy differences, but look closely, and you'll notice the disagreements were almost entirely regarding social issues like abortion and affirmative action, which inflame passions but have almost no economic impact on the guys who front tens of millions of dollars to finance these campaigns. The rest is cosmetic. Coke versus Pepsi.

Your choices in 2000 are almost certainly going to be Gore/Bradley vs. Bush/Dole, and I'm writing this more than a year before the first vote in the New Hampshire primary will even be cast.

But as the election approaches, the mainstream corporate media—which receives all that campaign ad money every time around—will tell you that you live in a functioning democracy.

Don't believe everything you see on TV.

Chapter Two

We Interrupt This Commercial
for the Following Press Release

You wanna find out the real media bias in this country? Set something on fire.

If you listen to talk radio, a lot of formerly gelatinous but now merely overweight radio hosts honestly think there's a pervasive lefty bias to the commercial media. As if the most prominent employees of people like General Electric and Microsoft are secretly reading Abbie Hoffman and Emma Goldman in their spare time.

Excuse me? Use your eyes and ears. When CNN stands for the Chomsky News Network, we can resume this discussion. Can you actually imagine Sam Donaldson or Tim Russert striking in sympathy with migrant workers? Not only are most pundits avowedly conservative, even reactionary radicals like Ollie North and G. Gordon Liddy, whose open contempt for the law is precisely what made them famous, routinely host national radio and TV talk shows.

Truth is, the real bias of commercial media is: *it's commercial media*. Giant media corporations make their money by selling ads to other giant corporations, and any long-term systemic bias exists because it serves that bottom line. Period.

That's why so many TV shows contain nothing but:

a) sex

b) violence

c) violent sex, and

d) occasional footage of pit bulls attacking fat people.

Not long ago there was a fire in a strip mall in the suburbs near my home in Los Angeles. And the Fox affiliate's 6 a.m. news show consisted solely of a helicopter shot of the burning building.

For an entire hour.

Like nothing else mattered in the world.

Apparently Beavis is now Channel 11's news director.

"Fire! Huh huh, cool! Huh huh, fire is cool, huh huh…"

After which Jillian, the weather chick, caressed the nation's midsection while wearing a really tight shirt. Then they went back to the fire.

Half these people probably think Edward R. Murrow is that actor who played Jaime Escalante in "Stand And Deliver."

So if you're an activist, next time you want your message to get TV coverage, don't waste your time coming up with fact sheets and compelling true stories. No one cares anymore. Really.

Just set fire to a half-dozen pit bulls, and turn them loose on some fat people having sex in the street.

Fox and CNN will arrive on the scene in about twenty minutes.

Just remember to tattoo the fat people with your group's message.

It's the only way to be sure what you have to say will make it into the final story.

Last year this guy stops traffic in Los Angeles and waves a shotgun around, so of course the TV stations drop everything and go LIVE to the scene. This is at about 3 p.m., just as kids are getting home from school.

Eventually the guy points the shotgun at himself, and suddenly a couple of thousand school kids have something new to ask mom and dad about.

And then afterward we have this huge debate: should TV stations have covered the whole thing, especially during an hour when schoolkids are just getting home?

And if the answer is yes: then should the TV guys have cut away before the suicide?

And if the answer is yes: then did they have enough time to see he was suicidal?

And if the answer is yes: then what do we do in the future to keep all this from happening again?

All of which is a bunch of rubbish, since this whole TV debate is accompanied by even more clips of the guy about to kill himself, which, if they're actually concerned about the questions they're asking, they wouldn't even be showing.

Media types often rationalize all the crap by saying that they're only showing us what we demand to see, and sadly, there's some truth to the argument. For example, ratings often double or even triple during live coverage of catastrophes and stand-offs with police.

I just don't see the allure. If I want to waste two hours of my life immersed in pain, despair, and misery, I'll just watch the L.A. Clippers. And I promise that in my radio segments, I'm taking the high road. You will never, *ever* hear me do a play-by-play of a police pursuit.

(Assuming none of you find out I'm actually a major terrorist and gunrunner known abroad by my sinister nom de guerre, Bob The Jackal.)

(Hmm. Well, I guess I let that out of the bag, didn't I? Damn.)

OK, anyhow, until the cops arrive, here's how bad things are getting:

Here in L.A. there's now actually a *paging service* where, for a nominal fee, every time there's a police chase you can get beeped, just so you can stop your own life cold, race home, and watch some poor panicking probation violator from Pacoima break the law until the law breaks him.

Just don't race home in too big a hurry. Or else the next show might start even sooner than you think.

The fact that we actually watch when the local news decides to become Faces Of Death is absolutely our own fault. But that doesn't mean that we can be blamed for all the other programming decisions as well. Corporate fealty to the bottom line also leads to conflicts of interest and censorship that we at home never see and rarely find out about.

In 1998, there was a flap concerning a set of TV ads that former ABC newsman David Brinkley taped for Archer Daniels Midland, the giant grain and energy company which calls itself the "Supermarket To The World."

(By the way, that slogan is apparently supposed to be a good thing, although it sounds a lot more to me like "don't screw with us; we've got all the food.")

The ads were controversial because they showed the former host of ABC's Sunday morning talkfest chatting up the virtues of ADM from a studio set that looked a lot like his old one. The ads were intended to air during the old program, which means if you were a casual viewer, you might not have realized you were looking at a commercial.

Which was the idea: ADM wanted to make their propaganda look like actual news.

That's bad, obviously, as no shortage of other jabbermeisters rushed to point out. Real newsmen aren't supposed to be lining their pockets by pretending a paid commercial announcement is actually objective reporting.

So ABC dropped the ads. Good for them.

But what nobody's pointing out here is that David Brinkley wasn't really doing anything all that different.

Fact is, ADM has been a major sponsor of all the Sunday morning talk shows, including Brinkley's, for years. And somehow, coincidentally, ADM gets a surprisingly wide berth.

For example, when ABC's experts talk about welfare, Cokie and Sam somehow never get around to mentioning the hundreds of millions of dollars in subsidies that ADM sucks up every year. And when the two Georges yammer about questionable financial arrangements with politicians, somehow they rarely get around to that condo in Florida that Bob Dole got through his connections with ADM.

Funny how that works out.

It's bad enough they've got all the food. Nobody ought to own the Supermarket of Ideas as well.

Here's an example of real bias in corporate media, the kind you usually don't hear about from the corporate media itself.

In Tampa, investigative journalists Steve Wilson and Jane Akre are suing their former bosses at the local Fox TV affiliate. Why? Because, their suit claims, they were fired simply for doing their jobs too well.

The reporters in question have a combined forty-four years of experience, three Emmys, and a National Press Club Award. The people they're suing work for Rupert Murdoch. Choose your side.

The series they produced concerned a suspected harmful substance in the milk supply: Bovine Growth Hormone, a synthetic hormone which cranks up milk production. Many farmers say BGH burns out the cow, and although the FDA approved the stuff a few years ago, some highly reputable labcoats worry it might lead to cancer in people who drink the milk.

BGH is banned in Canada and most of the European Union, but it's legal here in the U.S., where it's made by Monsanto—the same chemical geniuses who brought you PCBs and Agent Orange.

Wilson's and Akre's series outlined the growing health concerns about the additive, the consequences of which, they discovered, are already swishing around inside every jug of milk in the state.

You'd think the good people of Florida would get to hear what the hell they're drinking, right?

Before the story got on the air, a Monsanto attorney wrote an intimidating letter to the Fox higher-ups. Which should have been no big deal: truth is an absolute defense in libel cases. But the lawsuit says that Fox management buckled instantly, forcing the reporters to do dozens of increasingly distorted rewrites in an effort to appease the giant chemlords. Eventually, the story was killed and the reporters were fired.

If you want to know more, the reporters have placed the details of the case, including the text of the lawsuit itself and supporting documents, on their website at http://www.foxBGHsuit.com. The site also includes the reporters' version of the TV series and the phonied-up rewrites the guys in the ties apparently tried to get them to do. If you want to know how interviews and sound bites can be subtly framed to change the meaning of a story, this is an instructive case study.

When surveyed, about three out of four Americans don't want to drink BGH-produced milk. But thanks to Fox news executives, Tampa residents still don't know exactly what they're drinking. They have, however, learned a lot about house fires, car chases, and fashion trends on Oscar night.

Every real journalist in America should be interested in this case. After all, what's the news for, anyway—delivering you information, or merely delivering you *to* the advertisers?

One of my writer friends calls me last summer with a major scoop. Off the record.

He's all excited because he's working with Pulitzer Prize winner Seymour Hersh on a big story for Sy's new book. And ABC is spending major dollars preparing a big TV special on their findings. It's all very hush-hush, so I can't talk or write about it at the time, but it's *big*.

See, there's a guy in New York who says he found some papers after his Dad passed away. Dad was a big deal lawyer, and the papers are supposed to be a contract in which JFK paid Marilyn Monroe a whole bunch of hush money so she'd keep her mouth shut about their supposed affair.

This is the big blockbuster: JFK had sex. Possibly with Marilyn. And maybe he paid her off.

Well, it turns out that the JFK papers were forgeries. So ABC tries to cover their keister and look all journalistical by wheeling on their source and making *him* look as bad as possible. Class move.

ABC got suspicious because the typewriter technology that created the papers doesn't match the dates on the contract. Aha!

Good going, Sherlock. Let me again ask the same obvious questions I thought of in five seconds six months ago:

Why, exactly, would Jack and Marilyn put something they both wanted to keep secret *in writing?*

Duh.

And why, exactly, would they put a shady, secret, possibly illegal bribe in the form of a legal contract? What's the point? If Jack doesn't come up with the cash, Marilyn needs a legal agreement before spilling the beans?

Duh.

On the other hand, if Marilyn talks and hurts Jack's career, he's then gonna destroy himself completely by suing her in *open court* for the payoff money?

Duh.

This is what a Pulitzer Prize winner is doing with himself these days. Al Gore's having a Buddhist toga party in the Executive Office Building, and the Dean of American Journalism is going through thirty-five-year-old bedsheets.

Why? The bottom line is the bottom line: visceral images enhance shareholder value.

In short: they print all the news to give us fits.

Chapter Three

Don't Adjust Your Television Set...

Just Throw It Directly Out the Window

One fine Saturday night last summer, a lady friend and I put on our fancy clothes and went hobnobbing with a whole bunch of media bigshots in the Sunset Room of the posh Beverly Hills Hotel.

The occasion, you ask? Was I giving *Jeopardy!* buzzer tips to the Sultan of Brunei? Enjoying a bridge game in a bungalow with Charo and Merv, perhaps? Or just meeting George Michael across the street for a discreet chat?

No, my friends, the occasion was the L.A. Press Club banquet, a chance to sit and spit with hundreds of snazzy people who finance their cosmetic surgeries by showing car chases LIVE! and asking disaster victims to tell us how they feel.

Among these 250 people sat the very finest print and broadcast journalists in all of southern California. And about 240 other folks.

This was a cool deal. My companion and I got a free dinner, nursed our $5 soft drinks while furtively giggling at the cantilevered combovers surrounding us, and even got to watch a blooper reel of laughable news outtakes. Or it might have been a live feed from Channel 4. I'm not sure.

It wasn't hard to guess which folks worked in TV or radio or print. The TV people all had perfect voices and looked like fashion models; the radio people all had perfect voices; and the newspaper writers were also in the room.

The awards themselves are an illustrious, exclusive honor. They only gave out (and I'm not making this up) about *260* plaques and certificates.

Pretty much everybody in the room eventually went home with something. It was sort of like one of those self-esteem things for kids where Everyone's A Winner.

They gave me one for Best Radio Specialty Feature Reporting, which means my little commentaries kicked the ass of every gardening tip and bicycle safety announcement in the city. I'm honored and all, but then I think one of the washroom attendants got an honorary mention for Best Deodorant Cake.

There was one disturbing, revealing development, however:

In the category of Investigative Journalism by a major newspaper, the winner was...

Nobody.

Apparently there weren't even any serious entries.

Wow.

Somebody want to tell me again what a major newspaper is *for*?

I once had the temerity to suggest that maybe the world media was overselling their coverage of Diana Spencer's car accident just a teensy bit. I got plenty of angry email, but some new data has arrived to corroborate my position.

According to a British company that compiles newspaper articles by subject, the car wreck in Paris got more coverage in England than anything that happened in *all of World War II*.

In fact, Durants Press Cuttings—which has kept track of such things since the Bonapartes were driven from France—says that the crash and funeral got over twenty-five percent more daily coverage in Britain's major papers than the Nazi invasion of France, the withdrawal at Dunkirk, the bombing of London, the invasion of Normandy, or the final Nazi surrender.

Thank goodness Diana wasn't around during the 1940s. No one would have even noticed the war.

Leaving aside all the standard blather about the Liberal Media, it's important to remember almost every major news outlet in America is owned by one of a relatively small number of giant corporations, whose sole purpose for existence on this Earth is generating a profit for their shareholders.

Make no mistake: whenever your eyes settle for even a moment on any commercial media, *you* are the product.

And the financial interests of individual owners, and of individual advertisers who influence the reporting, have an increasingly negative influence on the quality of information you receive.

That's the bias everyone should see, but unfortunately, it's so pervasive that it goes completely unobserved, even by many media types themselves.

As to the news itself, it's also helpful to keep in mind that much of what passes for "news," especially concerning business, science, medicine, and even the environment, is based on press releases churned out by media flacks employed by other giant corporations.

Remember all the excited reports about the health benefits of antioxidants in green tea? Almost every major paper and many national TV news shows told you the following:

A recent study by a guy named Lester in Kansas found that green tea contains an antioxidant twenty-five times as powerful as vitamin E and 100 times more potent than vitamin C.

The magic ingredient is called EGCG, an abbreviation for epigallocatechin gallate, which if my Latin is still any good, translates roughly into "stand around the chicken and pray."

My Latin sucks.

Anyway, this is exciting news, right? Stuff that tastes pretty good might actually be a great way to prevent cancer. Let's hope it turns out to be true.

However...

If you read the fine print, Lester admits that the amount of tea that you have to drink is, so far, "not really...firmly established." Which means the amount you need to chug down might be a thimbleful, or it might be a gallon or more.

Granted, people in China drink more tea than we do, and they get less cancer. Cause and effect? Maybe, maybe not. There are other factors to account for—like the minor fact that they live in *China*, for example.

Who funded this state-of-the-art research, anyway? A company called Pharmanex. Pharmanex makes—you guessed it—plant-based health products. Which means Pharmanex just might, logically, stand to profit from a boom in sales of green tea.

Ohhhhh.

You want to avoid cancer? Green tea won't hurt you. It probably even helps. But you knew that yesterday. The real lesson here: press releases aren't the same as news.

Remember that big study saying that forty percent of men have trouble in the bedroom? Like maybe we could all do with a little Viagra now and again?

Well, guess who wrote it?

In February 1999, the *Journal of the American Medical Association* released a highly-publicized report providing conclusive, scientific proof that Americans are, in precise medical terms, a bunch of linguini weenies.

Practically every media outlet in the country ran with the story, since everybody loves this kind of news: if you do have trouble getting, er, perpendicular, it makes you feel like we're all in the same tiny little boat, while if you stand at attention at ease, shall we say, it makes you feel like captain of the ship.

There was just one minor detail about the study that the *Journal* neglected to mention: the labcoats who wrote it were also paid consultants to Pfizer, the people who make Viagra.

Oh, gee, there's a shock.

One thing that keeps a lot of people from buying Viagra is feeling ashamed to admit there's a problem…and all of a sudden out comes a study saying lots of people have the problem, so there's no reason to feel ashamed.

Coincidence?

Yeah, maybe. That doesn't mean the study isn't accurate. The authors were paid by Pfizer to review clinical trial data on Viagra before the drug was submitted for government approval. There's no direct connection to the study published in *JAMA*, and it's entirely possible that the scientists' financial interests in no way affected their methodology and conclusions. Let's hope and assume so.

But even so, the *Journal*, which was informed of the connection, should have disclosed the information about the researchers' previous work for the sex drug manufacturer.

If they had, the only medicine a lot of people would be taking as a result might be a big grain of salt.

Yeah, global warming will make the oceans rise and cause floods and wipe out coastlines and stuff.

But there's a brightside to global warming, and I don't mean just turning Nebraska into beachfront property. (And hey, ever wonder why the most famous investor on Earth, Warren Buffett, owns a house in Nebraska, and not on a coast? Maybe he just sees global warming coming, and figures as long as Omaha Beach is gonna be more than just a battlefield, he might as well get in on the ground floor.)

(And by the way, never confuse Warren Buffett with Jimmy Buffett. You don't want investment advice from Jimmy Buffett, unless you want to build your retirement nest egg around a truckload of margarita mix and a metric ton of cheeseburger meat. Which still makes more sense than some Internet stocks these days. Anyhow.)

The subject, you'll recall—and there is one, I promise—is the brightside of global warming. There's a group out there called the Greening Earth Society that actually says we should focus more on the *positive* effects of carbon dioxide. (You can find their rants through my webpage at www.bobharris.com.)

But while they claim to be environmentalists, do a little checking and reportedly they share offices with the Western Fuel Association, a bunch of coal companies, helping to *cause* global warming in the first place.

A lot of news is just somebody's self-interested press release, rewritten with a local byline that camouflages both the conflict of interest that originally created the story and the writer's woeful lack of effort in repeating it without looking for the conflict of interest.

In short, a lot of newspapers have more tools hanging around the office than Stanley.

Even so, there are lots of original stories in the paper every day. Surely those aren't written quite as haphazardly, are they?

Focus, Pinky, focus. Read closely, and you'll often find that even reporters at national newspapers often seem unable to understand their own stories.

Here's my favorite recent example, chosen for its sheer idiocy:

The USA Today—which as a source of news is sometimes just one notch above Colorforms—of December 14, 1998 carried an instructively bizarre and self-contradictory piece. Written by Daniela Deane, it hailed the "free market" imposed in Chile by Augusto Pinochet, that Grinchy-looking Eichmanna-be dictator dude who's about to go down for the small matter of killing off his opponents in large quantity.

Which, let's face it, is rude.

Granted, you could conceivably argue that creating one of the world's most inequitable ecomonies, albeit one that Wall Street can do business with, is worth the dismantling of a democratic society, the creation of death squads, decades of terror, thousands of disappearances, and the odd car bombing here and there.

Of course, that would make you amoral scum.

But you could conceivably make the argument. And make no mistake, a lot of the corporate press think that's a fair trade.

But let's leave that aside for a moment. Let's just get back to the USA Today thing.

It's taken as gospel here in the U.S. that Pinochet, who seized power in 1973 as the result of years of CIA assistance (something else the U.S. media ignores), was an avatar of the free market, a Latin American bulwark against state economic planning.

Which isn't entirely true, as Ms. Deane's story amply illustrates, not that she seems to have realized it. Her own story offered these illustrations of Chile's inspired free-market success:

a) Strict government control over banking, including constant audits and fines to keep bankers from getting greedy and making bad loans and going out of business,

b) a social security system where a ten percent investment is mandatory for all, and

c) laws requiring all investors to hold thirty percent of their assets in Chile for a year.

Excuse me? We can argue about whether these are good ideas. But one thing you can't argue: not *one* of these examples has anything to do with a free market.

In fact, they're all the exact opposite—government limitations and regulations precisely to *prevent* the abuses inherent in free markets. What Ms. Deane has done here is like pointing to Pamela Lee as an example of natural beauty. It just ain't so.

Did the reporter even bother to think about what she was writing? I'm not in her head and wouldn't want to be, so I won't guess. But for most business writers, it's a matter of faith that free markets are always good, that Chile's economy is good, Chile has a free market, and that Chile's economy is good because it has a free market. All of which are ludicrous oversimplifications.

Most Wall Street reporting is thickly dusted with similarly unhealthy bromides. But you don't have to be a University of Chicago economist to see the blatant contradictions in a lot of business news. You just have to be able to

a) read, and

b) think for yourself.

Which are two traits apparently not essential to writing for *USA Today*.

Part II

Sex, Race, Nationality
& Other Reasons to Hate Each Other

Chapter Four

Hottest Adult Pics!
Click Here!

Most people in talk radio think abstinence is a brilliant idea. And I agree: I think most people in talk radio *should* be abstinent.

For that matter, I think most people in talk radio should receive daily canings. But anyhow.

It's especially cool to get advice on trouser etiquette from somebody like Dr. Laura, who exudes all the sparkle and charm of a Catholic grade school nun and then suddenly shows up on the Internet displaying more pink than Owens-Corning.

As my comedian buddy Mike Irwin points out, Dr. Laura's sexual prescriptions, taken together, aren't exactly realistic. Like you're supposed to

a) remain a virgin until marriage, and

b) avoid marriage until you're mature, which

c) takes until you're at least thirty.

So…no one should have sex until they're thirty.

Not just with her. With anybody.

(Mike's a funny dude and one of my oldest friends. I used to live under his family's stairs when I was poor.)

(They knew about it and all. Not like that 1974 TV movie *Bad Ronald* or anything.)

Anyhow. Abstinence as a realistic approach to adult sexuality is often about as practical as using dry tinder to put out a fire.

I'm not saying you should drop the puck for a game of hip hockey with just anybody who owns a stick and gloves. I'm saying the reproductive drive is one of the three primal urges that preserve the species, the other two being: a) hunger, and b) wanting to pelt the Rolling Stones with chicken bones and burning tires for charging $200 a seat. Excuse me, but the Rolling Stones are a stronger argument for euthanasia than Dr. Kevorkian's games of Pin The Tail On The Forearm will ever make.

I digress. Anyhow.

Self-righteousness and hypocrisy only get you so far.

Unless you're a talk radio pundit. Then it's a good way to get rich.

Here's something that's way more fun than I thought it would be: getting an HIV test.

I was in a major relationship a while back. I'd say more, but I don't think either you or my publishers want me to turn this little space into The Personals.

ANNOUNCER: Welcome to 1-900-DO-ME-BOB. Here's the ad you chose:

SOCIAL OUTCAST: Hi, thanks for calling. I'm 2 foot 4, 319 pounds, with a beautiful blue eye and long blonde hair in several places. For exercise, I enjoy water polo, ski jumping, and sometimes just lying on my side and rolling down the street. I like to listen to Gaelic sea chanteys until my woofers blow, and my favorite way to relax is by playing with the chipmunks I keep in my overalls...

ANNOUNCER: If this person frightens you, press 1. If this person appalls you, press 2. To hang up and pretend you never called, press 3.

Beeeeep.

Actually, I'm being a little unfair to The Personals here. There are plenty of nice people out there, and they all deserve to meet someone they're really happy with.

Not me.

But someone.

Of course, if and when they and you and I all do make a love connection (hopefully not all at once)...this *is* the '90s. You need to *know* your health status, especially since any sensible partner-for-life will eventually turn into the East German border patrol and demand to see your papers.

So I went down to a clinic in Culver City and got tested.

Surprise #1: It takes all of ten minutes.

I'm amazed they don't have some sort of tie-in with an oil change place: you give them a quart, they give you a quart. Heck, they could start franchising the thing into a nationwide chain. Call it "Vein & Drain."

Surprise #2: Y'know who the biggest clients for some testing places in L.A. are? Porn stars. It's part of their job. These people get poked with needles almost as often as they get poked, uh, otherwise.

Suddenly I'm surrounded by a half-dozen laughably surgical mutant women with lips the size of an Eggo waffle, each of whom actually signed in with names like Venus Probe and Carnegie Melons.

Playing along, I unbuttoned my rugby shirt and suavely introduced myself as Richard Dangle.

Nobody got the joke. Everyone just called me Richard.

These people are 2400 baud, tops.

If you've ever wondered if porn stars are able to make any actual conversation between "Hi, did you order the pizza?" and "don't stand up until I get the last carrot out" the answer is No.

This was possibly the most amusing ten minutes of my life.

So get tested, OK?

Depending on where you live, you probably won't meet any of these synthetic fantasy lovers. But once the test is complete, you'll be ready when you finally meet the real thing.

Hooters—the bar where the sodas are bottomless and refillable and so is the staff—has opened a location near the popular and bucolic Santa Monica Promenade.

This has a bunch of local left-wing activists foaming at the mouth about sex and public morality exactly like they're, well, a bunch of right-wing activists.

And this in a metropolitan area that owes almost its *entire economy* to nubile young females titillating the yokels.

More pornography is created here in L.A. County than in the rest of the English-speaking world combined. Haven't these protesters driven through the Valley? The Van Nuys city motto is "Boom-chicka-boom boom, chicka boom, chicka."

Right behind my apartment on Melrose, there's now a forty-foot billboard of Pamela Anderson Lee Bono Allman Erectus. Pam's in a new TV show, although from the ad it's not clear whether she's a detective or a doctor or a coal miner or a chicken farmer, because frankly, the producers know it doesn't even matter. They could do a TV show with Pamela Anderson clubbing baby seals for an hour, and guys would watch. I'm surprised people don't just sell tapes of Pam staring vacantly into space for an hour.

Oh, wait, that's the one she made with Tommy.

But anyway.

If we outlawed everything that portrays women as sex objects, the Playboy Mansion would be in lockdown, Angylene would be breaking rocks, and Pauly Shore would get the chair.

Which sounds frighteningly like a Fox summer replacement comedy.

Anyhow, there's nobody to root for in this story that I can see. I don't know who's most pathetic—the Hooters executives who cash in on all the wiggling, the protesters shrieking over perfectly legal activity less offensive than the evening news, or the slackjawed losers with rib sauce on their mouths who actually go to Hooters thinking there's the slightest chance they're gonna score.

Dream on, boys.

Unless you're an elected official. In which case they probably deliver.

So Ellen came out. I still don't understand why this was big news.

We all knew that both Ellens—real and fictional—were gay for a long time, even though Disney made the poor girl hop in and out of the closet faster than Imelda Marcos in full slipper frenzy. The media buzzed for months with subtle clues proving Ellen Is A Lesbian the way a previous generation proved that Paul Is Dead. (Which he still hasn't admitted. The wanker.)

The real news here wasn't Ellen. It was us—no longer pretending that we don't know.

We straights are all aware that gay people share our schools, homes, and workplaces. But somehow a lot of us seem to hope that if we keep our eyes closed, maybe they'll all just go away.

When you're three years old, behavior like this is usually accompanied by putting fingers in your ears and screaming "Mommeeeeee!" Psychologists call this a "Neurotic Avoidance Reaction," although the U.S. military prefers the term "Don't Ask, Don't Tell."

Opening your eyes, however, reveals the obvious: gays and bisexuals are and always have been part of American life.

What would American culture be without the music of Cole Porter, the poetry of Walt Whitman, and the plays of Tennessee Williams? What would our history be without Susan B. Anthony and J. Edgar Hoover? Ironically, what would our image of masculinity itself be without James Dean, Rock Hudson, and Errol Flynn?

Contrary to the parroted PR that passes for reporting, Ellen Morgan wasn't even the first gay title character on network prime time. She's just the first we've agreed to acknowledge.

Sixteen years earlier, Tony Randall starred in NBC's "Love, Sidney," a series adaptation of a TV movie in which Sidney was openly gay. But no one watched, and it went off the air quietly.

Sidney Shorr's sexuality remained largely unaddressed. As NBC entertainment president Brandon Tartikoff explained at the time, "We have no plans of bringing it up, dealing with it, or mentioning it."

Or, more plainly: Mommeeeeee!

At least this was an improvement from the '70s, when Marcus Welby "treated" a gay man—by advising him not to talk about his "problem," stay in the closet, and start seeing a psychiatrist!

It should not be a radical act for Ellen simply to be who she is. What's the big deal, anyway? Why do we have difficulty dealing with friends, family, and even *fictional characters* whose preferences are never going to intersect with our own bedrooms anyway?

A recent study published in the *Journal of Abnormal Psychology* might have the answer.

In the study, participants filled out personality questionnaires before viewing a variety of erotic videos while wearing "genital strain gauges" to measure their arousal. (This is actually true, I swear. Obviously I went to the wrong college.)

Guess what? Turns out there's a striking, direct correlation between homophobia and latent homoerotic impulses. The very folks who revealed genuine fear or hostility toward gays on the written test were consistently more stimulated by gay images than heterosexual ones. Apparently, the myth is true: homophobes really *do* have closets to explore, or at least a desk drawer or two.

The rest of us are letting their ignorance influence us, for whatever reason.

So perhaps we should cease talking about gays and lesbians "gaining" mainstream acceptance, as if co-existence is entirely their responsibility. Instead, let's just begin thinking honestly and compassionately about our *own* motivations and phobias. I couldn't have been the only guy in high school who pretended to laugh at gay-bashing jokes just so the vicious ones wouldn't turn their venom on me.

Ellen didn't change; she just stopped pretending.

So should the rest of us.

Looking back at the whole Andrew Cunanan deal, something still bugs me about the way everyone discussed the case.

It's the phrase "gay serial killer."

Yes, Cunanan was gay, and yes, he was a serial killer. But why slam the two together as if they were related?

There's no justification for that, other than prejudice.

All the networks and major papers reported the rumor that Cunanan was HIV-positive and on some sort of Charles Bronson Death Wish-With-A-Swish thing, but that was only an unfounded rumor.

Reliable? Two words: Richard Jewell. Cunanan didn't have HIV after all.

So, um, he's a "gay serial killer" because his victims were gay? Nope. What about the rich real estate guy in Chicago and the caretaker whose car he stole? Not gay. Versace was gay, but there was no known relationship. So Cunanan killed more people randomly, as far as anyone could tell, than he did because of any sex preference thing.

OK, then, he's a "gay serial killer" because *he* was gay? Rubbish. The guy they convicted of the Atlanta child murders was black, and so were his victims, but no one calls him the "black" child murderer. And Ted Bundy was a heterosexual Republican who killed several other heterosexual Republicans. No one calls him the heterosexual Republican serial killer.

We don't know for sure why Cunanan killed anybody and probably never will. Which means that everyone's using a phrase with no grounding in reality that slanders an entire group of our fellow Americans, a group which already receives more than its share of hate crimes.

Cunanan's dead. Maybe we can bury our foolishness with him.

In the "Parents Alert" section of a recent Jerry Falwell publication, Tinky-Winky, one of the Teletubbies, has been outed as gay.

The shocking evidence:

Tinky-Winky has a big inverted triangle on his head.

The U.S. gay community often uses a triangle as a group symbol.

Tinky-Winky carries a magic bag.

Gays are often stereotyped as carrying purses.

Tinky-Winky is purple.

Which is sort of like pink. Not much, but sort of.

Coincidence? Jerry Falwell thinks not.

Then again:

The gay community also uses the rainbow flag and the Greek letter Lambda as symbols, neither of which appear on the show.

I live in West Hollywood and have never once seen a gay man with a purse, outside of the occasional drag queen in full Streisand mode.

And as to purple, on Earth it's more clearly associated with the British royal family, Welch's grape juice, and the Minnesota Vikings, none of which is particularly gay, although if you put all three in a hot tub you're halfway there.

So thanks to an immediate national outpouring of derision and common sense, Falwell had to distance himself from the article. Still, his spokesperson originally insisted that Falwell, who admittedly has never even seen the Teletubbies, was in full agreement with what his organization published.

Of course, you can take three or four isolated facts out of almost anything and use them to convince yourself of any point you'd like to make. As we'll soon see.

But first, let's back up. There are indeed good reasons to fear the Teletubbies. Homosexuality is not one of them.

In the Pre-fab Four's weird little biome, no clear line exists between the natural and synthetic worlds. Both real and man-made light are present; both real and man-made plants abound. Even technology and living flesh are merged, with technology clearly the dominant force. When the pinwheel spins and a TV signal is broadcast, the Teletubbies are helpless to resist. All they can do is stop everything, lamely protest with a futile "uh-oh," and watch passively as their own bodies respond to remote control.

Think about it. If George Orwell's 1984 had included children's TV, this is what it would have looked like.

Intentionally or not, an entire generation of children is being taught by example—before they've learned to speak, before they can even hold a single critical thought of their own—that domination from a monolithic media, controlled elsewhere by an insuperable power, is the natural order of things.

That's hardly a democratic vision.

Not that Jerry Falwell thinks critically about such things.

No, Jerry Falwell, man of God, spends his time thinking that the anti-Christ is a Jew, rock music is full of backward Satanic messages, and, according to the "Clinton Chronicles" videotape this holy man has enthusiastically hawked, President Clinton may very well command a sinister death squad.

And Jerry Falwell also thinks about sex.

Tinky-Winky has a triangle on his head. That's the secret symbol, see.

Right. The producers of the Teletubbies put a secret symbol *on top of the character's head.* That's how they're keeping it secret.

Don't anybody look at the character's *head,* shhh, it's a secret.

See, that's how gays communicate secretly. Giant triangles.

Delta Airlines? Gay.

The Kansas City Chiefs? Gay.

The Play button on your CD? Gay.

Fast Forward? Double gay.

But it's a secret. Don't anybody tell.

That way, only the really hip infants are gonna notice an eight-inch triangle on top of one character's head.

At least now when you catch your two-year-old reading a copy of *Blueboy,* you won't have to wonder how it happened.

Excuse me, but if Jerry Falwell and his evil minions are looking for sex in the Teletubbies, let me help out here:

Dipsy's the one with a *12-inch shaft* sprouting out the top of his skull.

What in the hell are Falwell's people looking at? See for yourself. Dipsy is the John Holmes of children's television.

It's enough to give a guy a serious case of Antenna Envy.

And that's not all. Check out little Po. Po's head is adorned with…yes, a perfect circle.

Hmm. What could this mean? Twelve-inch shaft…perfect circle…OK, you tell me what's happening on the other side of Teletubbie Hill.

In case you think I exaggerate: next time you're in a video store, pick up a Teletubbies tape and look at the cover. On the very first one I picked up, Po has her legs spread open as wide as possible, like a Hustler centerfold, but smarter-looking.

Coincidence?

Still, the character I really feel sorry for is the other one, La-La, who's stuck with that weird yellow spiral coming out of his head. What the hell kind of painful apparatus is that to go carrying around? La-La has either suffered a frightening impact to his spongy tissue, or that's a giant spirochete on the top of his head. No wonder Po never goes near him.

So, taking Rev. Falwell at his word, the Teletubbies secret code seems to be:

Tinky-Winky	gay
Dipsy	guy
Po	girl
La-La	diseased, possibly injured, asexual mutant

Finally, just to demonstrate you can pull things out of context to make any case you want to:

It's a fact that people who are unsure of their own sexuality often obsess about the sexuality of others, projecting outward their own innermost feelings. J. Edgar Hoover, for example, was certain everybody else in Washington had sexual habits worthy of blackmail precisely because of his own.

As noted earlier, clinical studies confirm that homophobes are often reacting to unresolved homoerotic feelings of their own.

So…is Jerry Falwell's interest in Tinky-Winky's sexuality really just his way of trying to tell us something? Is Jerry Falwell secretly gay? Consider the following…

Jerry Falwell's books include:

- *Church Aflame*
- *Stepping Out On Faith*
- *When It Hurts Too Much To Cry*

Jerry Falwell personally:

- has been voted three times as one of the 10 Most Admired Men in America—by *Good Housekeeping* magazine
- tried to put Larry Flynt, one of the world's leading heterosexual pornographers, out of business
- has never had sex with Jessica Hahn

And anagramming the names of Falwell's organizations, we find:

LIBERTY CHRISTIAN ACADEMY

Libertine days at rich YMCA

TRINITY UNIVERSITY MAIN CAMPUS

I'm a sly pervert in a muni city bus

LYNCHBURG BAPTIST COLLEGE

Pat…clench…bugger…Still, boy!

Ewwwwwww.

Clearly (and taken just as misguidedly out of context), Jerry Falwell is at *least* as great a danger to children as Tinky-Winky.

Parents Alert! indeed.

Aside to people who are angered by the preceding piece because they did not get the joke:

CAUTION: I am not actually saying that Falwell is gay. Please do not injure yourself or anyone else by holding that thought in your head longer than is comfortable for you. It is merely an ironic joke intended to illuminate his own faulty reasoning. Irony is an advanced concept and should not be attempted by the unready. If you do not get the joke, it is for the same reason that you think Falwell is a holy man. I cannot help you further. Please put this book down right now. Continuing to read might cause you to hurt yourself, others, or both.

Chapter Five

Can't We All Just Get Along?

And speaking of prejudice…

There's a place called Boone County in the mountains of West Virginia, all Mail Pouch signs and old coal mines. The people are as honest as they are hard-working, and they work too damn hard to be as poor as they are.

Boone County doesn't get a lot of visitors from down the hill. The ones they do get are often federal law enforcement types, so it takes a while to earn their trust.

They also have to deal with being considered stupid just because of where they live. Most of the folks down in Buckleyville—the big city in these parts—consider themselves superior, even though all most of them know about the mountains is what they've seen on *Hee-Haw*.

Strangely, there's also something of a language barrier. Because of their isolation, Boone County's soft southern accent is still decorated by Shakespearean-sounding Elizabethan phrases outsiders have trouble comprehending.

The challenge is cool—it's neat to be addressed as "thou" with a straight face—but when you realize they aren't just playing around and—gadzooks!—they really *do* talk this way, the effect is more off-putting than you'd expect.

Still, it's no huge deal. The Boonies, as they laughingly call themselves (even as others try to use the word as an insult) are as smart, funny, and kind as anyone.

Last year, I-62—the Senator Robert Byrd Highway—was completed, and everything changed. Boone County is now off Exit 47, just up the hill from a Stuckey's.

Roads lead to cars and buses. Recently, the mountain children began to attend Buckleyville's posh new Rockefeller Elementary.

Problem: the kids from Boone were as curious and creative as any, but because of the language barrier, their English scores were terrible. This in turn affected all of their other coursework.

One of the Buckleyville soccer moms spoke for many when she wrote a column in the local paper saying that Boonie kids "just don't want to learn," preferring a "tortured, degenerate gutter off-spring" of standard English. "Hopefully," she added, "they'll either have to learn right or go back where they came from."

Note how the grammar Nazi herself misuses adjectives, adverbs, and participles—all in one sentence.

Was an entire community of American children really failing, just because being born poor and in the wrong place makes you slow? Nope.

The simple problem was obviously the dialect: Buckleyville teachers just couldn't understand what Boone children said, and vice versa. Both sides tuned out.

Nobody's fault. Easy to fix.

Solution: recognize the differences, train teachers to understand the mountain dialect ("Boonic") so they can better assist the transition to standard English, and go from there.

Anything wrong with that? Of course not.

Except that Buckleyville and Boonic are fictional. Oakland and Ebonics aren't.

The difference is truly just skin deep.

At its heart, the Ebonics controversy had nothing to do with the best way to teach kids. The Linguistic Society of America, who would know, considered Oakland's plan "linguistically and pedagogically sound."

The only real problem here is that most white people just plain don't *like* the sound of black English, and those with race or class prejudices sometimes even assume that the speakers are lazy, stupid, or even speaking in a contrived anti-white code.

The poor phrasing of Oakland's announcement was also partly to blame for all the hoo-hah. Ebonics isn't a separate language, and by no means is it "genetically based." But most of what the school board was trying to say is true: it's a recognizable dialect with its own rules (true), primarily spoken by one ethnic group (also true).

It's not exactly encouraging to watch language professionals struggling to find the right words, but at least *someone* is trying to find a way to improve our urban schools that doesn't involve surveillance cameras and cavity searches.

Come on—you *really* think anybody in WalMartPlatz knows what poor city kids need more than the teachers who are right there in the room with them *every single day?*

Unless my study and my books be false, the argument you held was wrong in you.

(That's not Ebonics. That's Shakespeare. *King Henry VI*, Part 1, Act 2, Scene 4.)

I didn't keep the Camaros I won on *Jeopardy*. I felt really silly. I looked like a middle-aged guy in a red convertible trying lamely to pick up chicks.

Which is exactly what I was.

So I still drive a ten-year old car with 100,000 miles on it and only one headlight. It's teaching me a lot about race relations in this country.

And by the way, if you don't already know, I'm about as white as a Tic-Tac factory owned by the Promise Keepers: blond hair, blue eyes, pale skin that doesn't tan as much as it merely becomes slightly less pallid. Any whiter, I'm an Osmond. You need to know that to understand what follows.

See, my old car with only the one headlight is technically violating some safety law or another, which means I could get pulled over and hassled at any time. Y'know what? That headlight blew more than six months ago, and the police haven't batted an eye at me. I've driven past hundreds of cops in a dozen states, and I've never had a problem.

Most of my friends are white, and none of them ever say anything, either. It doesn't even cross anyone's mind. No big deal.

But darn if almost every black person I drive with—friend or new acquaintance, here in L.A. or on the road—doesn't immediately point out the blown headlight. In their world, driving around with one headlight is just asking for trouble.

Is it possible that their experiences with police are just a little different from mine?

Yup. A recent study looked at a random stretch of I-95 in Maryland, and black Americans were pulled over *five times* more often than their numbers would indicate. Similar studies have found equally racist attitudes in New Jersey, Florida, and all over the country. And supposedly the Justice Department is gonna do a big study, not that we need it.

The difference is so obvious you only need one light to see it.

What would you say if I told you that while Nelson Mandela was still in prison, there was a meeting of the 400 richest people in South Africa—and 399 of them were white?

You'd nod sadly and consider it an obvious sign of how bad South African racism was, right?

Well, suppose for a second it wasn't apartheid South Africa—it's Canada, right now. 399 out of the 400 richest people in Canada are white. You're probably thinking, wow, I thought they were a lot more enlightened than that in Canada. Oh, but wait. Canada didn't do the whole slave and Civil War thing like we did; they have a higher percentage of whites to start with. But still, 399 out of 400. Sounds like the hockey rink isn't exactly level. Yeesh.

OK. Now here's the real truth: it's not South Africa, and it's not Canada.

As this essay is written, *Forbes* magazine has released their list of the 400 richest people in America. Every single person is white. *Every single one*. Except Oprah Winfrey, who is so far down the list that Bill Gates makes her entire net worth more often than you probably cut your hair.

Without Oprah, the big money on the *Forbes* list is 100 percent caucasoid. Even including Oprah's millions—I did the math—the biggest fortunes in America are still more than 99.9 percent white.

Personally, I think the editors should re-check their numbers. I mean, racism *is* a thing of the past, isn't it?

A lot of people who read *Forbes* sure think so.

The very idea that individual races even *exist* is absurd on its face. Granted, to a five-year-old, the people of India might look different from the people of, oh, France. So a child, or David Duke, might be inclined to consider the cosmetic difference as something significant.

But where exactly on the map between India and France do you draw that line and say here's the racial divide? At India's border with Pakistan? No? How about between Pakistan and Iran? Iran and Turkey? Turkey and Greece? Italy? Woops, we're in France already.

You can't draw that line.

Not that supposedly smart adults don't keep trying. To people for whom a globe is too complex a device to operate, the differences between their neighbors of, say, Gambian, Irish, and Japanese ancestry are stark and obvious.

Remember *The Bell Curve*, the recent book claiming to show that different races have different levels of intelligence? It was a huge best-seller, the subject of countless TV chatfests and numerous thinkpieces in the mainstream press.

Too bad nobody seemed to want to notice the obvious: the book's own data directly contradicts its primary thesis.

Look: *The Bell Curve* ranks Asians at the top of the IQ totem pole, Europeans in the middle, and Native Americans at the bottom.

Excuse me? Native Americans are *direct descendants* of Asians— the ones who crossed the Bering land bridge. Their genes are so similar that *that's how we know they're related.*

Duh.

The fact that such illogical rubbish was considered so important tells you less about the book than it does about the pundits, many of whom are far less tolerant of the rest of America than they'd care to admit. One time in Pasadena I sat next to George Will at a TV critics' convention dinner. While waiting for the salad to arrive, George dove into a discussion of Ebonics by reciting a bit of Martin Luther King's "I Have a Dream" speech in a parody Ebonic accent.

Egad. I've heard more closely-reasoned sociological analyses on episodes of *The Jeffersons*.

Apparently George thought he was making a point. Possibly that he doesn't always think with his head.

Precisely.

Most of us, even intelligent, educated, well-intentioned people, usually don't think with our heads. Instead, we believe whatever helps us feel things we like to feel.

So ending racism isn't about talking someone out of hatred. You can't. It's about changing emotions. Gandhi was right: the only thing that defeats hate is love.

That, and maybe natural selection.

The Ku Klux Klan rallied in Jasper, Texas, site of the notorious murder-by-dragging. Some folks got all upset about the rally. Some folks think the Klan shouldn't even be allowed to assemble in Jasper.

But Jasper is in that humid, swampy part of southeast Texas, about as far south as Mobile, Alabama, but without the water. Do you have any idea how hot it is, especially on a June day in direct sunshine?

These idiots turned out in full Klan regalia, including the pointed white dunce caps—that's like seven or eight pounds of hot clothes and a suffocating headcover—in ninety-five degree heat and brutal humidity.

Neato.

If you want the Klan to die out, that's not something you protest; that's something you *encourage*.

The nearest heatstroke facility is sixty miles away. OK, you guys go ahead and rally as long as you like.

Hey, who needs Gandhi when you've got Charles Darwin?

Chapter Six

Foreign Policy
Stop the World, Washington's Gotta Get Off

Cuba

Give me your tired, your poor—but only if they can throw ninety mph with a good curve...

Apologies to Emma Lazarus, but that's apparently what ought to be on the Statue of Liberty these days.

The United States allowed a Cuban citizen named Orlando Hernandez and two of his friends into the country. They sent everyone else in their boat back to Cuba.

Why the special treatment? Because Orlando Hernandez was the older brother of Livan Hernandez, the Florida Marlins pitcher who kicked the tail ends of my beloved Cleveland Indians in the 1997 World Series. Supposedly, Orlando is an even better pitcher than Livan.

Thus the preferential treatment.

See, for all our talk about freedom and liberty and whatnot, it's standard U.S. policy to ship any Cubans picked up at sea right back to Cuba. However, when the Coast Guard caught this latest huddled mass yearning to breathe free, three of the group—and only three—were quickly granted entry: the pitcher, his wife, and a catcher he really likes. Everybody else had to go back to Castro.

(This just in: at press time, a new report has crossed the AP wire, stating that a fourth member of the group may be granted entry. Go ahead, guess why...Yup, it turns out he's a pretty good outfielder.)

Evidently, for all those Salvadorans and Guatemalans whom the INS sent home to dictatorships the message is: go home, unless you can steal it.

Guatemala

"If it is necessary to turn the country into a cemetery in order to pacify it, I will not hesitate to do so."
— Guatemalan President Carlos Arana, 1971

"The guerrilla is the fish. The people are the sea. If you cannot catch the fish, you have to drain the sea."
— Guatemalan President Efrain Rios Montt, 1982

"United States...support for military forces or intelligence units which engaged in violent and widespread repression...was wrong."
— United States President Bill Clinton, 1999

So President Clinton finally damn near apologized for America's role in almost a half century of repression in Guatemala.

Clinton was forced into this damn near apology after the UN's independent Historical Clarification Commission issued a nine-volume report called "Guatemala: Memory Of Silence."

Created as part of the 1996 peace accord that ended Guatemala's civil war, the Commission and its 272 staff members interviewed combatants on both sides of the conflict, gathered news reports and and eyewitness accounts from across the country, and extensively examined declassified U.S. government documents.

The result?

The UN's Commission concluded that for decades, the United States knowingly gave money, training, and other vital support to a military regime that committed atrocities as a matter of policy, and even "acts of genocide" against the Mayan people.

Thus Clinton's latest appalling damn near apology.

It's a common rationalization that in a civil war, both sides commit atrocities in roughly equal amounts. But the Commission examined 42,275 separate human rights violations—torture, executions, systematic rape, and so on, including 626 documented incidents the Commission described as "massacres." The final score:

93% were committed by U.S.-supported government paramilitary forces.

4% cannot be attributed with certainty.

3% were committed by rebels.

And worse, as Amnesty International and other independent observers have reported for years, the vast majority of victims were non-combatant civilians.

Merely trying to form an opposition political party was reason enough to be killed. So was being a trade unionist, a student or professor, a journalist, a church official, a child or elderly person from the same village as a suspected rebel, a doctor who merely treated another victim, or even a widow of one of the disappeared simply asking for the body.

But most of the casualties were Mayan Indians. Since the rebels didn't have the military strength to be able to hold cities, they hid in rural areas populated primarily by Mayans. So the Guatemalan government simply slaughtered entire villages, engaging in "the massive extermination of defenseless Mayan communities."

200,000 people died.

The Commission also concludes that massacres—which rose to the level of "genocide" during the war's peak years in the early 1980s—were not random acts of field commanders beyond government control. The genocide was deliberate policy. And U.S. support and training of the paramilitary was crucial, having "a significant bearing on human rights violations."

Unfortunately, the report doesn't name specific officers and government officials responsible. But that's not terribly surprising: last year, Roman Catholic bishop Juan Jose Gerardi issued a report on wartime atrocities that did just that.

A few days later, Father Gerardi was bludgeoned to death with a concrete block.

This is the country Bill Clinton now lauds, as "a battlefield of ideology that has been transformed into a marketplace of ideas."

Some marketplace. Ca-*chunk*. Thank you, come again.

Thing is, the Commission's findings aren't really news at all. What's new here is the depth of documentation, and that the information is coming from an official source.

That the Guatemalan military committed genocide and widespread atrocities has been widely known for many years. That the

U.S. supported and trained the Guatemalan military, along with repressive security forces in numerous other countries, is a matter of public record.

In September 1996, the U.S. Department of Defense admitted that manuals used until recently to train Latin American soldiers included numerous illegal practices, including summary execution. And in January of 1997, two CIA manuals on interrogation were declassified which contained plain references to electrical and chemical torture.

(One of the CIA's manuals, prepared for their 1954 covert war in Guatemala, is a twenty-one-page "Study of Assassination" which admits that murder "is not morally justifiable"—and then explains how to kill by whopping someone with "a hammer, axe, wrench, screw driver, fire poker, kitchen knife, lamp stand, or anything hard, heavy and handy." Which presumably includes concrete blocks. Yeesh. Scans of a few of the more bizarre pages and the complete text of the Assassination Manual are posted on my website, http://www.bobharris.com.)

However, the Pentagon's Inspector General characterized the manuals as simply "mistakes."

Yuh-huh. Sure.

The IG did not go on to specify just who made the mistakes or how, or why at least a thousand copies of the "mistakes" were distributed to police and military agencies around the world. And since the "mistakes" were made public, not a single American officer has been disciplined, reassigned, or even retrained.

In truth, the manuals can actually be traced to Project X, a 1965 Army program to train military, police, and paramilitary forces throughout Southeast Asia and Latin America. Project X was a direct precursor to Operation Phoenix in Vietnam and Operation Condor in South America, notorious programs with resulted in the deaths of tens of thousand of civilians. Project X was halted under the Carter administration, but its essentials were reinstated in 1982 under President Ronald Reagan.

And documents released the very same day Clinton wobbled through his damn near apology indicate that the U.S. was more intimately involved with the Guatemalan paramilitary than even the Commission report indicates.

(This new batch of documents was obtained by the National Security Archive, a non-profit bunch of truthseekers who do tremendous work obtaining and analyzing the internal record of things we weren't supposed to know. You can find many of their most intense finds posted on their website, http://www.seas.gwu.edu/nsarchive/.)

Thanks to the new releases, it's now indisputable that as early as 1966, officials from the U.S. State Department, far from opposing the torturers, set up a "safe house" for security forces in Guatemala's presidential palace, which eventually became the headquarters for "kidnapping, torture…bombings, street assassinations and executions of real or alleged communists." CIA documents also prove that from the get-go, U.S. intelligence was fully aware that "disappearances" were actually kidnappings followed by summary executions. Rather than act to stop the slaughter, however, the State Department continued to provide tens of millions of dollars in aid.

The flow of cash stopped briefly in 1977 when the Carter Administration made further aid dependent on improved human rights. However, once Reagan was elected, covert money and support for the Guatemalan dictatorship increased to new heights, as did the atrocities.

A newly-declassified Defense Intelligence Agency report states that, as was done by CIA-supported security forces in Argentina, the bodies of victims both dead and alive were routinely hurled out of aircraft into the ocean, removing "the evidence showing that the prisoners were tortured."

Still, aid to the Guatemalan government continued through the Bush years, even though CIA cables reported as late as 1992 on the continuing destruction of entire Indian villages, killing "combatants and noncombatants alike."

"Counterinsurgency" aid to Guatemala continued until 1995, when Clinton finally pulled the plug after American lawyer Jennifer Harbury was able to generate a small amount of public outrage over the torture and murder of her Guatemalan husband by a CIA informant.

Unfortunately, CIA "anti-drug" money continues to flow into Guatemala to this day. Not that it's serving any visible anti-drug function: as of this writing, Guatemala trails only Mexico as a transshipment point for Columbian drugs entering the U.S., and many of the same CIA-supported military officers suspected of human rights abuses are also considered to be major drug traffickers.

The State Department knows full well that at least 250 tons of cocaine pass through Guatemala each year. And the DEA reportedly has the goods on over thirty Guatemalan military officers. But so far, for some reason, prosecutions still aren't happening.

Gee, I wonder why...

Your tax dollars at work.

The 1954 coup destroyed Guatemala's democratic institutions and established a brutal military dictatorship as the nation's supreme power. And almost half a century of CIA-supported repression, torture, and murder later, an American president is barely able to mutter a damn near apology.

And people actually complain that Clinton isn't sorry enough about *Monica*.

Chile

While we're on the subject, let's fill in a few more details that you'll rarely find in the U.S. media. Go to any library and fish through the back issues of your local paper for stories concerning the recent arrest of Chilean General and Senator-For-Life Augusto Pinochet.

See how many of them tell you anything about U.S. complicity in his abuses of power.

And then start looking for information in places other than the newspaper.

As of this writing, Pinochet is still cooling his jackbooted heels in London, after the Spanish government requested British assistance in apprehending him for his involvement in the torture and murder of 79 Spanish citizens. The charges against Pinochet now include genocide, torture, and terrorism involving almost 100 people from Argentina, Chile, Spain, and Britain.

Usually, genocide and torture are considered bad things.

But several conservative commentators here in the U.S. have actually argued, alongside the current Chilean government, that the arrest is *itself* illegal, since Pinochet ostensibly has diplomatic immunity.

Hmm. I wonder how many of these same pieholes objected to the American military intervention into Panama to arrest Manuel Noriega. Unlike Pinochet, Noriega was never accused of direct involvement in the political murder of Americans. And unlike Pinochet's quiet detention, Noriega's arrest cost the lives of several U.S. servicemen, the lives of thousands of innocent Panamanian civilians, and millions of U.S. taxpayer dollars.

Here's another thing: American newspapers have front-paged the arrest and devoted entire pages to the legal case, often without once mentioning the entity largely responsible for the 1973 coup which brought him to power: the CIA.

That's no conspiracy theory. That's the findings of a 1974 investigation by the U.S. Senate Intelligence Committee.

Turns out U.S. intervention began as early as 1958, when the leftist physician Salvador Allende first came close to being elected Chile's president. Can't have that. So up to 100 CIA and State Department operatives were dedicated to an ongoing operation, "creating propaganda and organizational mechanisms capable of influencing key sectors of the population."

Pretty soon, the CIA began to bankroll *El Mercurio*, Santiago's leading rightist newspaper. Dozens of CIA radio messages linking Allende to everything from Stalin to the kidnapping of children were produced and broadcast daily. The CIA even stage-managed and underwrote expenses for Allende's political opposition in the 1964 election—as historian William Blum notes, at a greater cost per voter than LBJ and Goldwater campaigns spent here in the U.S. *combined*.

How come? Was Salvador Allende some evil pro-Soviet nutball, hell-bent on giving the Russkies a beachhead in the West?

Hardly. The CIA knew perfectly well that their propaganda about the pressing need to "save" Chile from Soviet influence was a lie. To quote from their own classified report, prepared within days of Allende's eventual election: "The U.S. has no vital national interests within Chile...The world military balance of power would not be significantly altered by an Allende government."

Fact is, the CIA knew damn well the Soviets didn't actually like Allende all that much, fearing another confrontation with the U.S.

like the one in Cuba. Allende wasn't even supported by many Marxists in his own country, who considered him too conservative.

So why the ruckus? Go ahead and try to find the evil in what the guy was doing:

Chile's new Popular Unity government began trying to deliver food, health care, and education to the poor. Allende, a medical doctor, also initiated a program to give free milk to poor children. In one of the most inequitable societies on the planet, the new president dared to advocate income redistribution to the poor, expanded trade with the Soviet Bloc, and, most worrisome, nationalization of Chile's enormously powerful mining corporations.

Aha. Wall Street was about to lose a few bucks. There you go.

Never mind that the dude was freely elected, followed the Chilean Constitution, and had the support of the Chilean people. Never mind that in spite of the CIA's best propaganda efforts, the popularity of Allende and his programs continued to increase. Never mind that the CIA's own analysis eventually showed no national security reason to proceed.

So the U.S. began an economic destabilization program designed to, in the words of CIA director Richard Helms, "make the economy scream"—a particularly brutal and pointless strategy, given that widespread poverty was *precisely* the major reason Allende was elected.

In addition, the option of a coup including the murder of Allende was also discussed in the Nixon White House as early as 1970, the year of Allende's first election. In preparation, the CIA assembled the names of dissidents worth rounding up, lists of which stuff the new regime would need to seize immediately in order to consolidate power, and other contingency plans.

And while aid and trade with the civilian sectors of the economy were largely curtailed, U.S. arms and funding continued to flow to the Chilean military, eventually making it the strongest sector of society, although the army's respect for law and the nation's integrity—what the CIA termed an "apolitical, constitutional-oriented inertia"—would have to be overcome. The CIA even began slipping anti-personnel and assassination weapons to more fanatical factions.

The game was on.

In 1973, shortly after Allende's re-election—gaining eight percent *more* of the public's support than he had in 1970—the Chilean
army marched. As the U.S. Navy and Air Force monitored the
action from just over the border, the country was essentially closed
off—much like Panama after the U.S. invasion—and potential
opponents of the new regime were rounded up and executed.

At least three thousand people shortly died or "disappeared."
Tortured and discarded, their bodies were reportedly hidden in pits of
lye, buried in mass graves, or even dropped into the ocean with their
bellies slit open so they wouldn't float and would never be found.

Tens of thousands more were imprisoned, the Constitution was
abandoned and eventually rewritten to permanently enshrine the
Generals' power, and the Chilean people learned quickly that
Pinochet's secret police, the DINA, was the law of the land.

Opposition wasn't even allowed outside the country's borders.
Coordinating with the intellignce agencies of other South
American dictatorships in "Operation Condor," the DINA contrived to eliminate even opponents living in exile throughout the
continent. In 1976, the DINA even staged the car-bombing assassination of dissident leader Orlando Letelier right on Embassy Row
in Washington, D.C.

Bottom line, here's what this horrifying price managed to buy
from Augusto Pinochet and his regime:

In Chile today, after seventeen years of grim dictatorship and
eight years of a government in which the killers and torturers retain
respect, power, and immunity, many Chileans are fully aware of the
sham democracy they live under. In some precincts, as many as
twenty percent of election ballots are turned in *defaced* in protest.

Twenty-five years after the coup, thanks to a quarter-century of
economic policies benefitting First World investors over the country's own citizens, Chile now has the seventh-most unequal distrib-
ution of income on Earth, tied with Kenya and Zimbabwe.

One-fourth of Chile lives in absolute poverty, and a third of the
nation earns less than $30 a week. Education, health care, and
other basic stuff that the citizens of most developed nations take for
granted are privatized, and so are about as available to the tin shan-
ty poor as a table at Chasen's.

This is the country the Clinton administration wants to include in an expanded NAFTA.

Not that you're gonna read the whole story in corporate media outlets that have rarely criticized the ongoing U.S. policies that helped create the situation. Some even question whether Pinochet belongs under arrest.

Believe it or not, the *Washington Post*'s editorial admitted that Pinochet overthrew a democratic government and killed thousands, but then actually added that "he also saw to the rescue of his country."

Excuse me? Rescue from *what?!?!*

Check your library's microfiches, and you'll find same sort of crap has been written about pretty much any CIA-supported dictator anywhere who played ball with U.S. corporations, no matter how high the body count: Suharto, Marcos, Somoza, the Shah, etc.

Too often, U.S. corporate access to a country's labor and export markets is defined as "freedom," no matter whether the locals can vote, organize, or even find enough to feed their kids.

Kosovo

BEGIN DIGRESSION

In the late spring of 1995, my father's lymphoma, which had been in remission, returned. Untreated, his life expectancy was maybe five years.

The first round of chemotherapy had weakened him. It had not cured him.

But *we have to do something*, said the doctors. And so they bombed him with more chemicals, even harsher ones than before.

Six months later I held his hand and watched him die from the side effects. The doctors offered no apologies.

They had done everything they could.

END DIGRESSION

The urge to do *something* in the face of horror is strong. You make yourself feel more powerful over things you can't control. But that doesn't mean what you're doing will actually help the problem.

It may only make things worse.

Here's a list of the countries the U.S. has bombed since the end of World War II, compiled by historian William Blum and posted on the ZNet website (http://www.lbbs.org/):

China 1945–46
Korea 1950–53
China 1950–53
Guatemala 1954
Indonesia 1958
Cuba 1959–60
Guatemala 1960
Congo 1964
Peru 1965
Laos 1964–73
Vietnam 1961–73
Cambodia 1969–70
Guatemala 1967–69
Grenada 1983
Libya 1986
El Salvador 1980s
Nicaragua 1980s
Panama 1989
Iraq 1991–99
Sudan 1998
Afghanistan 1998
Yugoslavia 1999

In how many of these instances did a democratic government, respectful of human rights, occur as a direct result?

Not *once*.

Depending on who you ask, territorial disputes between Serbs and Albanians go back to sometime between the end of World War II and 1389.

The Serbs consider parts of Kosovo historic national ground, much like the Alamo or Bunker Hill are to Americans. In recent decades, Albanians, often fleeing an oppressive government in their adjacent homeland, have become a large local majority.

Thus what is universally termed by the U.S. media the Conflict In Kosovo.

(Which, you'll notice, is increasingly pronounced "Kosova" by TV combovers and boob jobs. That's because they're mimicking the White House and Pentagon, who prefer the latter because that's how Albanians say it, thus transforming a single schwa sound into a show of solidarity with a people whose history, customs, and language they have no interest in whatsoever. Lame. But anyway.)

So it's hard to say exactly when this whole fracas started.

Exactly where bombing the holy crap out of Yugoslavia could have been averted is a little easier to pin down.

For years, the Albanians of Kosovo were led by Ibrahim Rugova, a Gandhi fan who practiced non-violent resistance.

Sounds like someone we'd want to hang out with, right? But Rugova—and the Albanians he represented—were completely ignored by the U.S. framers of the 1995 Dayton accords, which treated Slobodan Milosevic, who could have easily faced trial as a war criminal, as an essential partner in any future peace and stability. Milosevic's abrogation of Kosovar autonomy had occurred five years earlier, and Serbian repression of the Albanians in Kosovo was already underway and well-documented. But Rugova, the Albanians, and Kosovo were simply not a matter of U.S. concern.

After which, the KLA's armed solution made a lot more sense to a lot of Albanians. Which in turn gave the Serbs a rationale for increased security measures.

Conflict escalates...and here we are.

Is the U.S. (and its NATO figleaf) truly intervening for humanitarian reasons?

History very strongly indicates otherwise.

As has been widely noted, the U.S. did nothing to stop a death toll literally 100 times larger in Rwanda just five years ago. And in recent years, the U.S. has supported the people committing the atrocities in Indonesia, Columbia, Pakistan, El Salvador, and numerous other countries. Clinton himself admitted that the U.S. was on the side of the murderers in Guatemala.

We're supposed to believe that this time it's different. But at this very moment, Turkey, a NATO ally, engages in well-documented repression against its Kurdish population, with U.S. knowledge and support.

Reports of Serbian atrocities are heart-rending to any decent human being, but remember that the conflict in Kosovo was a simmering fact for years before it became a matter of U.S. concern. Similar atrocities committed by U.S. allies are ignored. And it has already been reported that the CIA was aware in advance that bombing Yugoslavia would lead to increased atrocities against the Kosovars.

And still the bombings began.

Why?

The primary goal of U.S. foreign policy after World War II, spelled out explicitly in numerous declassified internal memoranda, is the maintenance and expansion of labor and export markets to support the Western economic system.

Put simply: if it's good for Wall Street, then it's good, period. It's an ingrained, unquestioned knee-jerk assumption. The only debate among decision-makers is over how best to proceed within that paradigm.

The conflicts in Bosnia and Kosovo were never a major concern until they each led to large refugee populations that might move across national borders, where they might join with local minorities to alter the balance of local political power. Which doesn't make anybody happy. Greece doesn't need Macedonia getting all screwed up with an influx of Albanians. Turkey, Greece's historical enemy yet erstwhile NATO ally, doesn't need a nationalist leader arising in Greece in response, which would therefore threaten their security. And so on.

Which is why, in February 1999, the U.S. put a unilaterally-decided, quick-fix solution on the table at Rambouillet, France warning Milosevic we'd bomb the crap out of him if he didn't sign it. But similar threats were made early in the Bosnian conflict in 1994, and nothing happened. And the Rambouillet Accord included language allowing complete NATO occupation of all of Yugoslavia.

No carrot, no stick.

Needless to say, Milosevic didn't sign.

Anybody who plays poker knows you don't bluff if somebody's called your bluff successfully earlier in the game.

So now Madeleine Albright and Richard Holbrooke need to save face.

Kablooie.

So far [April 1999], the bombings have had the following effects:

As U.S. intelligence knew would happen, Serbian security forces have unleashed a brutal wave of violence against Albanian Kosovars. While a Serbian offensive was always considered likely, the bombings in no way have made any Kosovar safer. Instead, they are now endangered two-fold: both from the bombs and from enraged oppressors.

International observers—an acknowledged key to maintaining a standard of civilized conduct on the part of security forces—have been forced to leave the region, exacerbating the atrocities. Relief workers who might have been able to assist the victims have also been forced to leave the country.

Meanwhile, Milosevic's power is far greater than before. The Serbian population, under attack from a foreign power, has rallied behind their leader. Civilians are being killed in the attacks, and more deaths will surely follow, thanks to the country's weakened infrastructure. The survivors are angry. Which means the bombings have weakened Belgrade's political opposition—including Serbia's Democratic Party—into virtual non-existence. Any check on Milosevic's domestic police power no longer exists, and so while the people of Belgrade are weakened badly by the bombings, Milosevic will almost certainly survive the conflict vastly more in control than before.

Have we learned nothing from Iraq?

Peaceful negotiations—still possible only months ago—are now unlikely in the near future. A lasting peace has become almost unimaginable.

The likelihood is now greater that national minority/local majority populations across the region will be encouraged by the

U.S. action on behalf of the Kosovars to seek their own self-determination. Macedonia and Bosnia are now less stable than before. Russian intervention into the conflict, and the insanely dangerous possibility of escalation, has been treated as an acceptable risk. Washington has displayed its willingness to countenance a new cold war. The world is a more dangerous place.

As the bombing campaign fails to accomplish a single stated objective, the insertion of ground troops to become an occupying force with no end in sight becomes ever more likely. Which means protracted years of guerilla warfare, more destruction of the country under occupation, more refugees, and more deaths.

Have we learned nothing from Vietnam?

Back at home, the use of NATO as a beard renders the Constitution, already wobbly, a further weakened relic of a time when American citizens could expect their elected representatives in Congress to have some say in military affairs.

The Pentagon, which has pleaded for years for the capacity to fight full-scale war on two fronts simultaneously, finally has a two-front war (remember, we're still bombing Iraq) to call its own. Expect military expenditures to increase, even though the U.S. already spends more on defense than its top ten potential enemies combined.

Abroad, U.S. credibility among NATO countries for future operations—one of which may actually be necessary someday—is weakened. Greece and Turkey have never fully supported the bombings, and France and Germany are more reluctant every day.

Meanwhile, the UN Charter, a treaty signed by the United States, prohibits the use of force except in cases of self-defense or as authorized by the UN Security Council. Neither condition applies here. So once again, international law is revealed as completely meaningless to the United States, which bombs any country it wishes to with complete impunity. U.S. credibility in Third World nations is badly shaken.

And a dangerous precedent has been set: if international law means nothing to the sole remaining superpower, then international law means nothing.

So what now?

The bombing must stop. It is not meeting and cannot meet the campaign's stated objectives. It has, in fact, made things vastly worse for all concerned, including and especially the Albanian Kosovars.

Where we go from there should be determined not by Bill Clinton, the Pentagon, or NATO—none of whom have legal standing in the matter, as it happens—but by the UN General Assembly, which is where the issue of humanitarian intervention—if that was ever truly the issue—belonged in the first place.

(As this reached the printer, a peace deal: Serb troops withdraw; a UN force including NATO and Russia occupies Kosovo only; the KLA disarms; Kosovo remains within Yugoslavia. These are not the Rambouillet terms. NATO has quietly made concessions while declaring victory to the media. NATO's refusal to negotiate, leading to bombings which exacerbated Serb atrocities, is hardly vindicated. Do what the media won't: compare the current peace deal, Rambouillet, etc. yourself. You can find them at www.bobharris.com, with info for several relief agencies helping Kosovo rebuild.)

Iraq

Saddam Hussein is, no mistake about it, a bad guy. His government tortures and kills Iraqi dissidents. Saddam has invaded neighboring countries, initiating wars resulting in unthinkable slaughter. He may be stockpiling chemical and biological weapons.

Saddam Hussein is as bad a guy as real life offers.

So a lot of Americans think the United States should kill him.

For a while there, conservative radio dude Paul Harvey transformed his daily clot of folksy news items, half-true anecdotes, and Bose Wave Radio ads into a blood-curdling drumbeat calling for Saddam's head. Op-ed writers in almost every major newspaper openly called for the CIA to take action. On ABC's "This Week," even alleged liberals Cokie Roberts and George Stephanopoulos openly advocated Saddam's murder.

A lot of Americans need to stop going to stupid movies.

Here's why:

1) Political murder is precisely the sort of nasty habit that makes Saddam such a lousy fellow. It's deceitful and immoral for us to

advocate precisely the tactics America claims to be fighting against. Besides, political assassination is explicitly forbidden, both by Presidential directive and international law.

Not that anybody cares about minutiae like laws or ethics. Sorry. I won't bother you with that anymore. OK, let's move on.

2) The sheer hypocrisy of an assassination attempt on Saddam is downright surreal. Remember 1993? Bill Clinton bombed Baghdad in response to an alleged Iraqi plot to assassinate former President George Bush. So, using the White House's own reasoning, the open discussion of murdering Saddam invites and legitimizes any future Iraqi attack anywhere in the U.S. That's just begging for trouble.

Not that anyone cares about that, either. OK. Here's some more practical stuff.

3) Assassinating Saddam ain't exactly easy. People a lot closer to Baghdad than the Yaleies at Langley have been trying unsuccessfully for two decades. Most are now dead. It's not like Saddam's motorcade rolls past book depositories in an open convertible. Hussein lives and works in heavy military security. Assassination isn't even an option.

4) Supposing for a second that the CIA somehow gets an exploding cigar in the right palatial humidor, leaving behind even the slightest evidence of U.S. involvement would deal a crippling blow to American credibility in the Mideast.

Several pro-Western governments, notably Egypt and Algeria, are already weakening under the pressure of growing Islamic movements, and much of the Arab populace supports and admires Saddam. So the murder of Hussein would further destabilize American allies and solidify anti-Western political parties.

5) And even if the CIA *could* kill Saddam and leave no evidence, who exactly would replace him? It's not as if Baghdad is teeming with pro-American activists steeped in democratic traditions and backed by military force. The death of Saddam would lead simply to another dictator, one with even more reason to fear and loathe America.

Meanwhile, the power vacuum after the killing would provide Iran and Turkey an excellent opportunity to strike against their

Kurdish rebels currently in Iraq. Which means lots of extra bonus death and instability. There's just no upside here.

Bottom line: Saddam's not a target, no matter how cranky Paul Harvey gets.

OK, so if the U.S. can't just go and shoot Saddam, America can always invade and kick butt, right? Nope. Here's why:

1) As mentioned, the coalition of 1991 is long gone. Russia and France want Iraqi oil. Many Arab countries are on the sidelines or opposed to military action. Even Kuwait waffled when the subject of invasion was broached.

2) Even if the U.S. does invade, what exactly is there to attack? This isn't 1991, with the retreating Iraqi Army trapped on the road to Basra, ready to be carpet-bombed into skulls and cinders. Iraq's Army isn't amassed on a front. It's not even amassed. It's dispersed all over the country. The Iraqi Army ain't the target this time.

The target here is Iraq's cache of chemical and biological weapons, carefully hidden in various places around the country. Since random genocidal bombings are out of the question, there's really nothing specific the U.S. can attack, other than anti-air installations and warplanes that fire in response.

3) And even if the Pentagon knew exactly which weapons existed where, military action near any actual CBW storage facilities would inevitably risk the release of bad bugs, killing unpredictably large numbers of innocent people.

Granted, the American media probably wouldn't care about a bunch of suffocating Iraqis, anymore than they cared about the people of El Chorillo in Panama City. But in any release, U.S. troops would also be at major risk. And that's politically unfeasible. Remember Gulf War syndrome? Anthrax kills in days, botulinum in hours, and VX within minutes. You ain't seen nothing yet.

Bottom line: there's no way to invade, there's nothing to bomb, and success means disaster. So forget about any Gulf War sequels for now.

OK, so that means we're all gonna die, right? Nope again. As always, the media's need for drama has made things sound a lot worse than they actually are.

First, some good news: British and U.S. weapons assessment reports on Iraq estimate that Saddam may—*may*—have a half-dozen or so chemical or biological weapons stashed away somewhere. That's bad, but it's not the same as full-scale production, which spy satellites would easily detect.

And what Saddam *doesn't* have is a delivery system: at most, Iraq might have enough parts on hand to patch together a couple of short-range missiles and maybe wipe out an Israeli or Saudi city. But even then, such an attack would require weeks or even months of preparation, during which time human or satellite intelligence would provide sufficient advance warning to allow diplomatic or military response.

Finally, the best news of all: according to the intelligence assessments, Saddam still has no known ability to attack the U.S. or Europe. It would take Iraq at least four years to create a long-range missile, and such work would again be detected long in advance.

In short, Saddam is ruthless blue scum, but he's just not that darn menacing. Contrary to what various lunatics say on *Crossfire*.

OK, show's over. Not a normal American movie, was it? Big build-up, no climax, bad guy lives. Roll credits, everybody drive safely. Thanks for coming.

Of course, with all the flashbangkapowie at our disposal, there's always a chance the good guy might still try to kill off the bad guy once and for all.

Let's just hope the writers figure out that stupid movies rarely lead to smart foreign policy.

India

OK, so the Indians tested the Bomb.

I'm referring, of course, to the India Indians, the ones with the Ganges and the Gandhi and the Aloo Gobi. Not the American Indians. If the American Indians had the bomb, *then* we'd have something serious to worry about.

If the American Indians had the Bomb, we'd be on our knees just praying that all that casino money hasn't been pooled together to get some payback for the blankets with the cholera. The best deal Clinton could probably cut would be to give up Cleveland. Which is fair, what with the Chief Wahoo thing and all.

But not to worry. The American Indians don't have the Bomb. Thanks to toxic waste dumping upwind of their reservations, they've got plenty of radiation, but they don't have the Bomb.

The India Indians have the Bomb. And that's a problem, certainly, but let's not overreact. Everybody knew they had the bomb. India got the technological potential for the basic parts to the Bomb Home Game a full decade before any of us got cable. And we know which one has done a lot more damage so far.

OK, so Pakistan has to run a couple of tests in response. They pretty much have to, for the same reason pickup trucks in Texas have a gunrack: you don't get carjacked when you're obviously packing. But that doesn't mean they're planning to drive into the bad part of town.

Let's get a grip here. It's nice to daydream that the fall of the Berlin Wall was the end of the nuclear era, but that has never been anything close to the truth. Which is why the G-8 turned down Clinton's calls for sanctions against India.

(The G-8, by the way, isn't a vegetable drink. It's the leadership of the eight leading industrialized nations. Which probably still includes a lot of vegetables, especially if Yelstin shows up.)

The G-8 is comprised entirely of active nuclear powers, except for: a) Canada, which is too polite to nuke anybody anyway; b) Japan, which already got blowed up real good; and c) Italy, which doesn't make any bombs, and as you know if you've ever driven an Italian car, we can only thank God for that.

So there's good reason why the G-8 cocktail won't swallow sanctions on India: it would be ludicrous on its face. Look around. The French tested weapons in the South Pacific just a few years ago. The Brits and Russians aren't blowing things up, but they're still doing research on how. And the U.S. leads the world in ongoing nuclear development, spending billions of dollars every year on computer simulation tests that are almost as good as actual kablooies.

The Lawrence Livermore labs are only a few hours' drive from where I sit here writing this. And still the newsclones nearby are furrowing their brows, pretending that India and only India is responsible for the continued existence of a nuclear threat.

Hey, the U.S. implicitly threatened to use nuclear weapons in Iraq just *three months* earlier, and suddenly we get all preachy when somebody else just runs a test. Doesn't anybody ever remember anything anymore? Is three months too much to expect?

Of course, if we elected our public officials for having good memories, they wouldn't have to keep telling proscutors that they can't recall.

China

So. Clinton went to Beijing, reviewed the troops, chatted with students, and debated with the head Red.

Excuse me for asking something most folks think has already been answered, but why was Clinton there, anyway?

Clinton and Jiang Zemin have agreed that:

a) pointing missiles at each other is a bad thing,

b) talking more about Tibet might be a good thing, and

c) reasonable people can agree to disagree, even over a masscre of unarmed students.

The missile deal is good news, but no big thing. It's acknowleged as something that would have happened with or without Clinton's China visit. And without verification, which is barely even discussed, it's pretty much meaningless.

The Tibet thing sounds like good news, and unexpected at that, but don't get excited. It's still just talk, entirely within the existing assumption than Tibet is part of China, and Jiang's so-called conciliatory gesture actually added a new condition for further open dialogue: Tibetan acceptance that Taiwan, which just held independent, democratic elections, is also subject to Beijing's rule.

If Jiang was actually serious about peace in Tibet, he probably wouldn't be adding new ground rules. And he'd probably do something about that small matter of China's 1000 or so Tibetan political prisoners.

Yeah, but the trip represents a real breakthrough in Chinese openness, right?

That the Chinese government allowed an impromptu Clinton/Jiang debate to air on national TV is generally considered sensational, especially given Clinton's open mention of both Tibet and Tiananmen Square. Western op-ed writers all blithered wishfully about this Chinese glasnost as a harbinger of impending democracy.

Swell, but let's consider the obvious: Jiang had no way of knowing what Clinton was about to say. And given that Clinton had already shown himself willing to bite his tongue—reviewing Chinese troops, head high, on the site of his hosts' most notorious massacre of unarmed democracy activists—Jiang might well have believed that Clinton would continue to play along.

So was the live broadcast actual self-scrutiny, or temporary screw-up?

Let's look at what has happened since: China's state-run newspapers barely even mentioned the exchange, and several omitted the discussion entirely. In a later appearance, when Clinton said he was about to depart from his prepared remarks, Chinese state television pulled their own plug, returning only when it was clear that his digression was nothing but boilerplate about the environment.

Around the country, Chinese security forces continue to try to shut down pro-democracy internet sites, pro-democracy activists continue to be rounded up, and private citizens who merely try to *speak* to foreign journalists continue to face arrest.

Yeah. Real breakthrough.

Leave it to American writers to think you can change the world with a single TV sound bite.

Make no mistake: China is changing, and fast. But not because of anything a U.S. politician might say; because of what the corporate power behind that politician might offer.

BEGIN DIGRESSION

Speaking of what's behind the Clinton trip, if you listen to American talk radio nutballs with any frequency, you've already heard that the President went to China mainly to report in with the Home Office. The buzz, in rough form, is generally that Johnnie

Chung was a conduit for payoffs which influenced White House approval for the transfer of sensitive satellite technology to China, thereby endangering American national security. And therefore Bill Clinton is guilty of treason.

Obviously, some technology may have been stolen by China, and that sucks. But too bad there's roughly zero evidence to support blaming that all on Clinton, not that *that* stops anybody these days.

The fact is, the Chung money is small potatoes, the DNC gave it back, and there's precious little to link that cash back to China. Even so, the timing for a bribe doesn't work out, this particular technology transfer is trivial, and most military folks say national security is in no way threatened. Oh, and Reagan and Bush both authorized similar transfers as well.

So basically, it's a good story, except every component is false.

But don't expect that to stop an intrepid reporter. Particularly a crazed zealot employed by Rupert Murdoch.

By this time next week, Matt Drudge will probably be telling us that Monica Lewinsky is a Chinese agent, and her exotic sexual prowess—honed by years of Manchurian Candidate training in Beijing's secret complex of erotic hypnolabs far beneath Beverly Hills—is what sealed the deal.

A Fox TV movie will surely follow, starring Melrose Place's Tiffany Amber-Thiessen in the lead role, and featuring Pat Morita as Kang, her evil controller. Look for Kang action figures, manufactured in Hong Kong, in stores in time for Christmas.

Welcome to the New World Order.

True story: at a college gig last spring, I spent ten minutes detailing the various allegations surrounding Johnnie Chung. An hour later, in the Q&A session, I discovered that one student thought I was referring to Cheech Marin's partner, and another thought I meant Maury Povich's wife.

Sometimes I wonder why I even bother.

END DIGRESSION

Granted, Clinton delivered some quality lip service about human rights, which sounds good to us homefolks in a mid-term election year. But read the overseas press. A big chunk of the rest of the planet just ain't buying it.

Let's look again at the credibility of our President as an avatar of social progress before the world.

Last time I ran the numbers, the six leading jurisdictions in executing their own people, per capita, were China, Iran, Iraq, Nigeria, Florida, and Texas. Bill Clinton himself once signed a death warrant on a retarded man who was so unable to understand his situation that he saved some of his last meal for *later*. And Clinton dares to lecture about human rights.

In my lifetime, in Asia alone, the government Clinton represents has supported brutal dictatorships in Indonesia and the Philippines, armed drug-running paramilitary groups in Afghanistan and Laos, and bombed the holy crap out of Cambodia. And still Clinton dares to lecture about human rights.

At the very moment you're reading this, U.S. shoe and clothing manufacturers are avoiding U.S. minimum wage laws by employing Asians, many of them kids, in appalling conditions. According to one of Nike's own internal audits, leaked to a UN auditor last November, thousands of young Vietnamese women working at one of Nike's largest plants received $45 for working 267 hours a month.

Do the math. That's not even seventeen cents an hour, working continuous sixty-three-hour weeks, in a plant where the levels of a known carcinogen were more than 175 times higher than even Vietnamese health laws allow. The U.S. government barely bats an eye.

And Bill Clinton dares to lecture about human rights.

So *of course* when Clinton tries to talk street with the students at Beijing U., the result isn't a boxers-versus-briefs MTV lovefest, it's Ohio State University East. Big shock.

The trip's not about human rights, folks, or the guy wouldn't go strolling through Tiananmen Square. It ain't about democracy, or the leader of the Free World wouldn't be consenting to *anschluss*—explicitly agreeing, in an unprecedented announcement, that the 21 million people of newly-democratic Taiwan are destined to be ruled by the Beijing police state.

It's about money.

Not 100 yards from where Clinton paraded before the Chinese army, there's a Kentucky Fried Chicken franchise three stories high.

Welcome to the New World Order.

It's not just that China quiere Taco Bell. Multinational telecommunications, banking, textile, and even military and nuclear technology companies are lining up for the main buffet.

The U.S.-China Business Council's executive committee includes the chairmen of Boeing, Eastman Kodak, Federal Express, Honeywell, and numerous other corporations, many of whom saw Clinton's trip as a key chance to expand their piece of the action. At the very moment Clinton dined separately with Jiang for the cameras, White House cabinet members and economic policy advisors listened as the Business Council's director extolled the virtues of opening the Chinese market.

Wall Street smells a billion new customers.

Whether or not those customers can vote is utterly immaterial.

So while Clinton vogues for the press, guess who Commerce Secretary William Daley and the rest of the crew are meeting with all day? Read *their* itinerary. It's not exactly brimming with political prisoners and human rights activists. Daley's rolodex is a roll call of potential investors, middlemen, and franchisees.

This ain't about getting China's government to open up to the Chinese people. It's about getting China to open up to multinational corporations.

Clinton's goal, as he himself confirmed on a radio call-in show in Shanghai, is simple: the eventual integration of China into the World Trade Organization.

The WTO is the NAFTA-on-steroids supranational corporate body that seeks to ordain the rights of multinational corporate trade as more powerful than any individual government or citizenry.

Clinton's so horny to get China into the WTO that he even surprised his own advisors by characterizing China as an "emerging economy." Those words carry a specific meaning: if Clinton's version of reality spreads, then under WTO standards, such a designation would mean that China needn't even play according to the same rules as developed nations. China would be able to maintain tariffs and protect local industries; competing nations—pretty much the rest of the industrialized world—could not.

Here's what that would mean to us: if you live in a factory town, you won't much longer.

After the radio call-in show, Clinton toured Shanghai's glistening new $150 million stock exchange, where he again called for China's entry into the WTO; afterwards, he attended a roundtable talk with Chinese entrepreneurs, and spoke at a breakfast meeting of American businessmen cashing in on the fast-growing market.

Clinton also called for permanent Most Favored Nation trading status for China, in spite of Beijing's status as a major weapons exporter. Clinton's claimed negotiating victories aside, China has curtly declined to sign an international missile non-proliferation agreement that the White House hoped might be a centerpiece of the trip.

Here's an example of how destabilizing the weapons trade can be: China exports missiles to Pakistan, and it's the fear of Pakistan and China that caused India to test their weapons in the first place, which in turn caused Pakistan's test in response.

As a result, Clinton looked good for us home folks by slapping trade sanctions on India and Pakistan.

So consider the bizarre Asia policy the White House now constructs, in the wake of China's flat refusal to contribute to regional stability:

a) sanctions for the people buying from and defending themselves from Beijing, but

b) permanent MFN status for China itself.

Clinton was also originally scheduled to stop at Shanghai's massive General Motors plant, which cranks out 100,000 Buicks a year, for sale in the U.S. at high profit thanks to cheap labor—at least until GM workers in Michigan began their well-publicized strike, in part to protest precisely the very export of American manufacturing jobs that Clinton's (and the GOP's) policies so visibly promote.

The trip to the Buick plant was cancelled, apparently so the two stories wouldn't appear on the news together.

Back here at home, if Clinton's opponents can stop obsessing about BJs long enough to talk *coherently* about White House China policy in terms of campaign financing—beyond their weird theories about how Johnnie Chung was manipulated by the evil Kang— fine: who do you think gave the the Democrats the *real* majority of their soft money?

Nike's multi-billionaire CEO Phil Knight once hosted a fundraiser that generated more cash for Clinton in a single *night* than Johnnie Chung, Cheech, and Connie did in their entire lives. And, gee, it's probably complete coincidence, but somehow you don't hear Clinton saying much about Nike's factories in China and the rest of Asia.

The ARCO folks just cut a $70 million methane exploration deal on this trip that could eventually be worth up to $1.7 billion. And, golly, ARCO's access to both Chinese and U.S. officials instrumental in the deal probably has nothing whatsoever to do with being one of the Democratic Party's largest contributors.

Boeing has just announced a deal to sell up to $1.2 billion worth of aircraft to the Chinese government. Citicorp is cutting banking deals. Aetna is selling insurance. Westinghouse should soon close a deal to sell nuclear power equipment.

Welcome to the New World Order.

So if this is the real deal, why doesn't the GOP blow the whistle? Check the FEC records. Because they're paid for by many of the same people.

You want to understand Clinton's trip? As Deep Throat told Woodward and Bernstein, on the trail of the last great trickster to visit China:

Follow the money.

Part III

DC Comics

Chapter Seven

Monica
What I Saw Under a Table in the Hallway at the Revolution

Are you now, or have you ever been, a member of an enjoyable party?

Henry Hyde once said that by having sex with Monica Lewinsky, Bill Clinton "damaged his office."

Wow. That's what I call vigorous.

I hope *I* have that kind of ability when I'm fifty. Geez.

Anyhow.

Am I the only one who was so amused by this motley assortment of known adulterers, hypocrites, and closet white supremacists accusing the President of lacking in moral fiber? Excuse me, but this couldn't be the U.S. Congress—it's more like the second act of *Deliverance*, with Bill Clinton as Ned Beatty, and Bob Barr chasing him around trying to make him squeeeeal like a pig.

Call it Jenny McCarthyism.

Oh, wait, excuse me, it wasn't about sex. Yeah, right. Never mind a bunch of panting Congressmen getting all sweaty over the testimony like the whole scandal is a Snap-On Tools calendar and Kenneth Starr's referral is a big box of Kleenex.

Supposedly, the gripe about Clinton was perjury—that he rose his right hand when maybe all he was really raising was his finger.

Maybe so. And gee, if we let our politicians get away with lying, why, pretty soon we'll all be jaded and eventually we'll feel like really powerful people have way more influence than we do, and guys like me will even get paid to tell jokes about it just so we can all feel better.

Well, thank goodness we can nip *that* in the bud.

But if this whole proceeding was, as the GOP claims, about the truth, the whole truth, and nothing but the truth, then riddle me this, Batman:

On January 7th, 1999, at 1:30 p.m. Eastern Standard Time, every single member of the Senate raised their right hands and solemnly swore that they would, quote, "do impartial justice," so help them God.

They *swore under oath* not to prejudge the case—to have an open mind and consider only the evidence presented and nothing else.

But we all know that's simply not honest.

There are only a handful of Senators whose votes were ever in doubt. We *all* already knew how almost every member of this jury was gonna vote, long before the trial began.

(And by the way, look it up: within moments of the swearing-in, partisan bickering forced a recess before even the first order of business.)

Obviously, most Senators did *not* have an open mind.

Which means (and help me if I'm missing something here) pretty much the whole Senate has sworn under oath to something that wasn't true.

Forgive me for expecting a shred of reason or consistency, but if that's grounds for removal from office, there's a *prima facie* case that the entire U.S. Senate is now unfit to serve.

Then again, Clinton does have the right to be judged by a jury of his peers.

We've all heard a gazillion opinions about whether pursuing a trial without the slightest chance of conviction was or was not a waste of the public's money.

From the way I phrased that, you already know my opinion.

Polls say most of you agree. But a lot of people still want to return America to the 1950s—a time when if you wanted to have sex with an assistant, you had to be Director of the FBI.

Anyhow, everybody on both sides of the aisle yammered about the richness of the pomp and the majesty of it all, and that's all fine. But there's one thing that made it impossible for me to take any of this seriously: the little shiny thingies on William Rehnquist's sleeves.

Most people assume that Rehnquist gets shiny thingies because he's Chief Justice. But the Supreme Court isn't *Star Trek*. They don't do that. You can look at all the pictures of Supreme Court justices you want. You won't find anybody else with shiny thingies.

So what's the deal?

Truth be told, William Rehnquist is really into Gilbert & Sullivan, and in Rehnquist's favorite production of one of their operettas, there was a British Lord Chancellor character who had gold thingies on his sleeves. And so William Rehnquist decided he wanted to wear them, too.

That is so…*dingy*.

(Incidentally, the character Rehnquist is so inspired to emulate lusts for his teenage ward and fathers a child out of wedlock. Damn. Ain't life grand?)

I just can't take impeachment seriously when the presiding judge is halfway dressed for an audition of "Pirates of Penzance."

Dude, you're the Chief Justice of the Supreme Court. You're not Rex Smith. Get a grip.

I mean there's a principle here. If Rehnquist gets to wear his little shiny thingies, where do we draw the line?

Suppose David Souter really likes the little logo thingie on the chest that makes you a crew member of the Enterprise. Would he get to wear it on his robe?

Or how about if Clarence Thomas wanted to dress like a Klingon, or Sandra Day O'Connor wanted to wear Ferengi ears? How is that so different?

Hell, we could give up the title Supreme Court altogether, and just call them the Deep Space Nine.

At one point, former Presidential candidate and possible Martian spy H. Ross Perot announced that President Bill Clinton is mentally unstable.

Cool.

"This guy's brain's not working correctly," Perot said, just before ducking behind the podium to look for any of those anti-Castro Cubans who might still be trying to disrupt his daughter's wedding.

Look, conceding that the little Martian guy might be right—I mean, if *this* is the kind of behavior we wanted in the White House, we might as well have elected Hugh Grant, with the added bonus that the entire far right would begin having seizures—but still, excuse me:

Since when is stability a requirement for political power?

I mean, Clinton's no prize, but come on, presidents are almost always a little nuts. You gotta be just to want the gig.

George Bush had that whole twitchy hyperthyroid thing, spending half his term zipping around in high speed cigarette boats and jogging laps around the east coast and pounding Halcion and denouncing vegetables at random and bombing third world countries and struggling to hold a single thought long enough to construct a coherent sentence.

Granted, Bush never had a sex scandal, but look, do you really want to give the nuclear button to somebody who plays *golf* on the dead run?

And what about Nixon? You want instability? The guy made Enemies Lists, for crying out loud. That's just not normal. You don't do that in the White House, you do that in a shack in Wyoming. I'm surprised they never found polaroids with people's faces X'ed out in lipstick. At least Nixon never bombed anybody. Other than Cambodia.

Some of our most important leaders had *huge* problems. Lincoln was severely depressed and his wife was completely nuts. J. Edgar Hoover had that whole cross-dressing thing. Ben Franklin was such a horndog he probably would have tried to seduce Hoover.

Look, Jimmy Carter was as stable as a water molecule, and who misses his presidency?

Stability is fine. But if I've gotta choose between stability in the Oval Office or my own, my office wins every time. Which is why Clinton came out of the whole Monica shindig eight points *ahead of* Reagan's average approval rating (look it up) and about fifty points ahead of Ross Perot.

Although these days if Perot accuses Clinton of having an old lady in the attic, we might actually have to listen.

Far be it from me to defend the Clintons, many of whose policies I detest (as regular readers know), but is there indeed a bias to the way scandals are reported? You decide:

Linda Tripp announces that George Bush had an affair with one of his secretaries.

No outrage.

Linda Tripp announces that Bill Clinton had an affair with an intern.

Swarms of reporters.

Linda Tripp's secret recording of conversations with Lewinsky—which definitely occurred—is, plainly, a felony in direct violation of Maryland state law.

No outrage.

The leaking of the tapes to the media, thereby obstructing justice by preventing the independent counsel from securing Lewinsky's testimony via standard legal procedures is itself, plainly, a direct violation of federal law.

No outrage.

The President is accused of a sex act which is, plainly, not a crime.

Swarms of reporters.

And so on.

Look, I'm as titillated as anybody else by the prospect of Clinton and Lewinsky getting a little Executive Action.

But the stills from her yearbook and graduation have been burned into our skulls more firmly than our own high school memories. (I remember thinking at the time: are those the only two photos she ever posed for? There are more and better pictures of alien spacecraft.) Finally, somebody found five seconds of Clinton actually hugging the girl, which we still see highlighted and looped and running back and forth like an illicit Cat Chow commercial.

The mind staggers at how much truer a democracy we could have—if only our reporters spent one-tenth this much effort examining campaign contributions, the performance data of our weapons systems, and the fine print of tax proposals and international trade agreements.

Until that day comes, we'll just have to settle for fancy graphics and theme music built around a White House intern stimulating the President below the waist.

And every time we turn on the TV, some producer is trying to do the same thing to us.

Look, I don't approve of pornography. Not at all. Oh, I enjoy it, mind you, but I don't approve.

(Just a joke for a cheap laugh, honest. And besides, even if I once did enjoy shining the staples, I actually had to read the entire Starr report cover to cover. *Blaugh!* I might not get perpendicular again until Christmas. Not that Christmas makes me perpendicular. Oh, dear. Moving on.)

And I certainly don't approve of—or like—much of what Larry Flynt publishes in *Hustler* magazine. It's degrading to women, men, dogs, houseplants, the paper it's printed on, numerous other inanimate objects, at least a half-dozen classes of subatomic particles, and several philosophical concepts in a variety of languages.

At least as far as I know. I bought exactly one copy when I was in college, out of curiosity. And the only word I can use for the contents I found is: "primitive." *Hustler* definitely puts the "og" back in pornography.

Then again, that seems to be Larry Flynt's entire point.

Which means that criticism, frankly, isn't going to change anything. And if I have to live with either Larry Flynt's version of the First Amendment or Jerry Falwell's, that's not even a question. So I can deal, whether I personally like it or not.

Besides, I actually met Larry Flynt once, a little over a year ago at a UCLA Book Festival. And my own level of personal amorality was remarkably unaffected.

OK, the word "met" is an exaggeration. To be more exact, I once engaged Larry Flynt in several minutes of idle chat while standing twelve feet away with my body turned to one side, so in case anyone I knew walked up—particularly any women I might ever want to speak with again—it wouldn't really look like I was standing there talking with Larry Flynt.

To set the scene: the UCLA Book Festival is an enormous outdoor event where thousands of pasty-skinned readers, none of whom ever leave the house, venture blinking mole-like into direct sunlight for the opportunity to swarm dozens of pasty-skinned writers, none of whom ever leave the house. A Pallorpalooza, if you will.

Deepak Chopra was there, signing copies of *Headless Body, Mindless Time*, promising readers a lifetime of natural, holistic health. Which doesn't explain why his hair looks like melted vinyl. Dude puts the "goo" back into "guru." Just a few steps away, Arianna Huffington was teaching young girls how to preserve themselves in formaldehyde and maintain self-confidence in spite of being bright orange.

And not thirty yards away from these two obvious space aliens, I arrived at a third: Larry Flynt, sitting in his wheelchair, gold chains around his Jabba-like neck, smiling beatifically—with absolutely no one going anywhere near him.

This was a surprise. I would have thought he'd get at least a little attention, ever since Woody Harrelson played him in that movie, *White Men Can't Jump*.

(Relax. If you can't make that joke about Larry Flynt, there is no hope in the world.)

I almost felt sorry for the guy. Almost. And besides, how often do you get the chance to meet someone whose bizarre obsession with chronicling illicit sexual activity has become a part of American pop culture? Outside of Ken Starr's grand jury room, I mean.

So I sidled closer.

We talked about the weather.

I wasn't seen.

Time cut to the present. Larry The Hutt has offered no less than a million dollars to anyone who will come forward with proof of an adulterous relationship with a member of Congress or other prominent national official.

Granted, he's talking about *past* affairs, but then again, this is Larry Flynt here. Get the goods next week, and he's not gonna turn it down.

Which means the cloakroom walls now have ears. And how likely is it that a million bucks is all the incentive some Monica manquée in a Senator's office needs to drop trou on the next pizza run?

Wouldn't you? I've never personally slept with an elected official, but come on. A million bucks? It's tempting.

So really, if you think about it, what Larry Flynt has done is put a price on the head (loud clearing of throat here) of every national official in America. A booty bounty, in essence.

Which also means that if you were in office right now, there's no way you'd even *think* about starting an affair. Every single second, you'd wonder if you were on Candid Camera, C-SPAN, or the Spice Channel. (All of which are becoming remarkably similar these days.)

Which means it's remotely possible, then, that thanks to this period of crazed right-wing sex-baiting Jenny McCarthyism, Larry Flynt, of all people, may be doing more to maintain the personal morality of this country's leaders than anyone else.

Ick.

———————————

What exactly constitutes "sex" anyway?
Personally, I think it's

a) anything you do naked, that

b) makes you say any word more than five times in a row.

Thing is, the perjury shindig in D.C. really balanced on where and how we define the word "sex." If you consider the hard palate an erogenous zone, then you probably think Clinton committed perjury. If not, not.

But does it make sense that the definition of "sex" most of the media accepted unquestioningly is the one provided by Clinton's accusers, most of whom regard as sin any oral skill beyond speaking in tongues? That's like choosing between AOL and Earthlink by asking the Amish.

Ultimately, whether or not Clinton committed perjury rests largely on whether *his* definition of "sex"—which excludes tonsil hockey—is or is not credible to typical Americans.

But hardly anybody's even asking *us*.

So the *Journal of the American Medical Association* published a study on exactly that question.

And surprisingly, the survey found that sixty percent of college students, male and female, do *not* define power flossing as "sex."

Then again, seventy percent of college students define beer as a food group. We still need more information.

But the point is, Clinton is clearly not the only person with a limited definition of sex. Which makes the claim that his definition is unique—and therefore he committed perjury—a little weaker. It would be interesting to survey the rest of America and see what we think.

But don't hold your breath. The AMA responded by firing their editor, after seventeen years of highly respected service, just for printing the survey.

They say the *Journal's* not supposed to be political. Rubbish. They've injected themselves happily in political debates ranging from the abortion debate to the JFK assassination.

Is it more likely, perhaps, that the editor dude got fired because the AMA doesn't want to screw up the efforts of their dozen-plus lobbyists working to curry favor with the GOP Congress?

Apparently, the AMA leadership spells the phrase "physician, heal thyself " with an h-e-e-l.

I don't know whether Kathleen Willey told the truth on 60 *Minutes*. I do know something about the class bias of columnists in the corporate press.

That said, did she?

Arguments for: Bill Clinton has definitely cheated on his wife and lied for political gain on numerous occasions, the latter of which is a far more serious (although sadly common) offense against you and me. Clinton has also begun a Nixonian series of stonewalling tactics, although so far as we know he doesn't have Howard Hunt breaking into Kenneth Starr's office or G. Gordon Liddy planning to kill reporters at the *Washington Post*.

Arguments against: Willey's friend Julie Steele says that Willey put her up to lying to corroborate the story. (And saying so got her indicted by a vindictive Kenneth Starr.) Willey is in major debt and has tried to trade her story for a book deal that would cover that debt, and the publisher involved says her story keeps evolving. And Executive Shrew Emeritus Linda Tripp, whom Clinton's opponents consider credible in the Lewinsky matter (and who I'm becoming convinced is actually Howard Stern playing a big joke in drag), claimed that Willey didn't seem distressed by whatever encounter occurred, but "happy and joyful."

So who's telling the truth? I dunno. Neither do you. You might think you know, but only two people actually do, and neither one is particularly credible.

In this respect, it's similar to the Paula Jones thingy. Which is obvious enough that even major syndicated columnists were able to pick up on it and start comparing the two.

OK, then, so who's more credible—Paula Jones or Kathleen Willey?

Keeping in mind that people usually choose their beliefs not because of any objective evidence but to provide themselves with desirable emotions, it's not surprising that Paula Jones has op-ed writers split evenly down ideological lines. Most of the media's wealthy conservatives prefer to believe her, while the media's wealthy moderates (usually mislabeled as "liberals," even though almost all actual liberals were long ago dispatched from corporate newspapers) prefer not to. And in discarding Jones' charges, derogatory references to her class status—e.g. "trailer trash"—are common.

On the other hand, Kathleen Willey received unanimous support from conservative columnists and reluctant credibility from many moderates. Even feminist icons like Anita Hill and Gloria Steinem constructed worst-case contingency rationalizations for their continued support of Clinton if the charges proved true.

In short, Willey is widely perceived as more credible.

Why?

It's not because Willey's story is more provable than Jones'. There's no direct physical or eyewitness evidence for either, and he said/she said often falls apart in court when, as in both cases here, the plaintiff has demonstrably changed her story. Both Willey and Jones were seen shortly after meeting Clinton and reportedly seemed pleased. Both have sought to cash in. Both may still be telling the truth anyway.

Still, as you've no doubt heard, numerous pundits and talk-show vanity cases continue to state that the latest crisis damages the Presidency more than the others, because Willey is the first *credible* woman to charge Clinton with sexual misbehavior. And that's just flat wrong, since Clinton has now already admitted under oath that Gennifer Flowers, another non-ruling class "bimbo," was telling at least some truth.

So what exactly makes Willey so different in the brain of a talking head? Simple—money.

Kathleen Willey *is* the first of Clinton's accusers to come from the same economic stratum as the pundits themselves.

In the days after the *60 Minutes* interview, I saw at least a dozen TV commentators bluntly awarding credibility on the basis of appearance, and another half-dozen print hacks referencing Willey's presumed "class." And I wasn't even looking for it. CNN's Bill Press even praised the details of Willey's clothing accessories—specifically admiring her lovely "pearl necklace."

Real convincing choice of words in a sex harassment case, Bill. Puh-leeeze.

Indeed, whether or not she's telling the truth, Paula Jones eventually underwent a complete pre-trial hair, wardrobe, make-up, and orthodontic makeover—all merely so she can simulate upper-class carriage and therefore *look* like she's telling the truth.

There's something truly horrid implied in all this: that upper-class women are more truthful and deserving of respect than lower-class women—that higher social position equals greater honor.

It doesn't.

But it's precisely this false assumption, correlating social station with personal worth, which facilitates the abuse of power—*including sexual harrassment.*

Whether or not Clinton actually did the stuff he's accused of, it's clear that most of the trenchcoats and hairpieces yakking about it remain content to live in a climate that only encourages more of the same.

Y'know, the President's exploitation of women might be even worse than you think. And not because of anything President Plum did to Miss Scarlett with his Lead Pipe.

My problem with Clinton (and the GOP) has more to do with economic policies—particularly the turning of American labor into just another global commodity—which work really well for people who own stock, and really badly for people who wheel stock around.

Whatever Monica Lewinsky did or didn't do in the Study to Mr. Boddy with his Candlestick, the sad fact is, Monica's chores were pretty much the only job Clinton has created for low-income women since he was elected.

Remember Welfare Reform?

In 1996, trying to appease right wingers in an election year, Bill Clinton signed a bill eliminating Aid to Families with Dependent Children for hundreds of thousands of struggling Americans—the vast majority being women, many single mothers trying to raise children. This was despite the brutally obvious reality that plenty were already working—albeit at minimum- and low-wage jobs, often under the table just to get by. ("Under the table" is meant here strictly in the payroll sense, of course. Get your mind out of the Oval Office.)

Meanwhile, Clinton's support of international trade agreements has made lower wage jobs harder to find, and the weakening of health and safety rules have made those jobs harder on those who find them.

And for those who don't find jobs, one final irony: welfare laws now include strict provisions requiring unwed mothers to establish paternity, which means providing welfare officials a complete inventory of their sex lives. In many cases, they have to specifically recount to a judge when, where, how often, and with whom—precisely the details which Bill Clinton refuses to provide himself.

Let's stop worrying about what Clinton did to one girl in his study, and start paying attention to what he (and the GOP Congress) has done to millions of other American women—right on top of his desk.

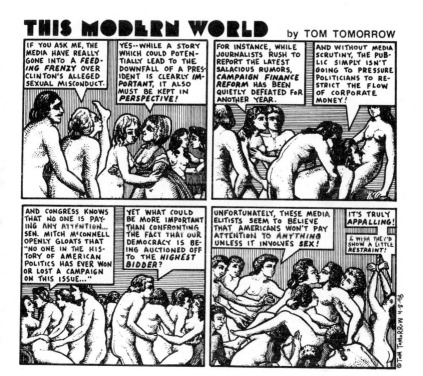

Metaphorically speaking, of course.

So far.

If you believe ABC, almost one quarter of the entire United States sat down and watched Barbara Walters make Monica Lewinsky weep.

This skillful extraction of bodily fluids in extreme close-up for public titillation, of course, is what Barbara Walters does for a living. Watching her manipulate the guest into crying is the highlight—the money shot—of every interview Barbara Walters does.

Barbara Walters is the Jenna Jameson of the tear duct.

And none of this is news.

Afterward every media outlet from *Nightline* to frat boys writing words in the snow from hotel balconies opined about Monica's cloths, hair, and lip liner. Body language was analyzed. People on the street were interviewed. Poll numbers were compiled. Sides were chosen.

And none of this is news.

(Incidentally, several of my best friends and I discussed what we would honestly do if any of us were President of the United States, and Monica Lewinsky had suddenly dropped trou, exposed her great white caudal fin, and snapped a mercenary thong in our direction. And we all agreed, sincerely, on exactly what we would do next: *call security*.)

As to what Clinton did that night, all you probably heard was that he ducked out to New Jersey. Commentators speculated he was trying not to be asked about the blubberfest. The wire services noted that he was seen singing along with Gloria Gaynor's rendition of "I Will Survive."

And not one minute of any of this is news.

What Clinton was actually *doing* in New Jersey *was* news: attending a fundraiser for Senator Bob Torricelli that pulled in two million dollars in a single night.

And this is money for a guy who isn't even up for reelection until 2002.

That that's normal now—*that's* news.

That just for a shot at some Senate seats you gotta raise over ten thousand dollars a day, seven days a week, for the whole six years you're in office—*that's* news.

And that the news media doesn't even think it's unusual enough to bother reporting—*that's* news.

Too bad Monica didn't mention it, so it might have gotten on TV.

Chapter Eight

Campaign Financing,
or I Wish My Vote Mattered More, But Then Charlton Heston's Would, Too

Texas is the only state in America even weirder than California.

This is a cool culture: near Dallas, I was once passed on the freeway by a Lexus with a gun rack.

That's what I call a real man.

Texas is full of things you won't see anywhere else.

They don't talk about it much, but if you go to the Texas Capitol building in Austin, walk right straight down the front steps, keep going straight down the street in front of you—that's Congress Street—and stop at the first bridge you come to…you're dead center over the lair of the largest urban bat colony in America.

The Austin Chamber of Commerce doesn't advertise it much, but there are tens of thousands of bats living underneath the Congress bridge, and just before sunset on summer nights, they all come out at once in a giant cloud that is easily the weirdest and coolest thing I've ever seen.

One minute, there's a beautiful sunset on the water, and the next minute, you're immersed in a 100-foot wide ribbon of solid batwings.

They keep pouring out for about ten minutes, until the ribbon of bats blots out a chunk of sky all the way to the horizon.

Yee-hah!!!

That might sound sort of scary or creepy to stand in the middle of, but it's actually really neat. The bats navigate well enough not to smack into you, and they wouldn't bite if they did. So what you get for your time is a quick peek into a whole vast dark world that's always there, even if nobody wants to look at it. Cool.

I was surprised at how few of the locals bother to see the show. There's no souvenir stand selling rubber bats wearing cowboy hats or anything. But everybody in Austin knows there's a big pulsating mass of creatures underneath Congress. It's just that nobody wants to talk about it.

I can't think of a better metaphor for politics in America.

If we're going to make this country a functioning democracy someday, we'll all have to work up the courage to wade into the darkness and shine a light on some stuff we'd rather not see.

But take heart. The swarm of lobbyists and hidden donors in our capitals may be scary to look at, but if I can handle 30,000 bats, I'm pretty sure the rest of us can handle a bunch of Yale grads.

Although the bats are definitely less creepy.

According to an Associated Press computer analysis, among Congressional candidates who entered the last two weeks of the race with the most financial resources—meaning money already spent and money still available, combined—*ninety-six percent* won.

Ninety-six percent.

And it gets worse. In almost sixty percent of House Of Representative races, winning candidates had a financial advantage of at *least* ten-to-one.

No wonder pro wrestlers are getting into politics. It's the only other major sport that's so obviously fixed.

It ought to tell us everything we need to know that in 1998 the only significant victory by an independent—out of over 500 major political races nationwide—was by a professional wrestler. And if "The Body" can get elected, how long will it be before motocross, tractor pull, and drag racing champions start jumping into public office? TUESDAY TUESDAY TUESDAY!

Make no mistake—voting is the essence of democracy, absolutely indispensible and fundamental. But it means *nothing* without an informed and active electorate whose activities ensure a genuine choice at the ballot box.

Women didn't get the vote in America because men changed the laws out of the goodness of their hearts. Women got the vote because they marched and protested and fought for the vote, literally for generations.

Civil rights in the South didn't happen because of a walk to a voting booth, but because of a March On Washington.

And so on.

Democracy isn't just about who you vote for in November. It's also about what you do in the eleven other months of the year.

Even as early as December 1998, the policy auction we call the 2000 presidential election had already begun. It'll take at least $20 million just to compete in the primaries. That works out to about sixty grand a day, every single day.

At this rate, the only people in office in ten years will be NBA power forwards and the geeks who own Yahoo!

The only Democrat with access to those kind of dollars is Al Gore. End of story. The GOP won't make the illegal fundraising allegations stick because both sides of the aisle have more dirty money than Papillon.

The rest of the mule team—Gephardt, Bradley, Kerrey, Kerry, Wellstone, etc.—have about as much chance at the nomination as Vinny Testaverde has at winning a Super Bowl. One of these five will probably be the VP.

I'm inclined to pick Bill Bradley, because he's tall. Seriously. Tall candidates do really well in the TV era. Besides, he hasn't done anything for the last few years, so he's prepped for the job.

Meanwhile, the only GOP candidates with a financial prayer are Steve Forbes, George W. Bush, Lamar Alexander, and Newt Gingrich. Liddy Dole has an outside shot if and when she gloms the hubby's rolodex.

Quayle, Bauer, Ashcroft, Kasich, and a half-dozen GOP governors are just kidding themselves. Their poll numbers make the new *Avengers* movie seem like a runaway hit. Cripes, if they're gonna do something for vanity's sake, they really ought to just mosey on down to GlamourShots and pose a few for the missus. Same impact on history and they throw in the frame for free.

Bush *fils* is the current favorite, but his straw-poll performance will decline rapidly once he exists as more than a name outside of Texas. Besides, there's supposedly a chance he won't even run because of rumors about his, um, er, *active*, uh, personal life, which apparently only recently finally began to resemble that of a properly unsatisfied Republican. Evidently Bushboy has more ass to cover than Dr. Laura. Still, if Bush runs, the nomination is his.

Lamar Alexander can't win, because I sat behind him on a plane a while back and absolutely no one recognized him, even though we were flying into Tennessee, where he used to be the governor. The guy's harder to remember than the last time "The Family Circus" was actually funny.

Newt Gingrich can't win, because he has a public approval rating only three points ahead of having a weasel running loose in your sinuses. Besides which, he owes Bob Dole bigtime for the tobacco-money rescue on last year's ethics fine, which means if Liddy runs, Newt will probably have to support her campaign. Assuming he isn't too busy feeding on carrion.

Which leaves Steve Forbes. And since most Republican partisans have no problem with paying retail for government office—the use of private wealth to attain public authority is seen as a First Amendment right—there's no reason Steve Forbes can't win the nomination, except for the fact that he strongly resembles one of the Budweiser lizards.

Forbes has unlimited wealth, a tax plan which appeals to the fiscal conservatives, and a newfound hard line on social issues that plays well with people who speak Tongues as a second language. He'd be the perfect GOP candidate if his eyes weren't on different sides of his head.

So...

The early guess for 2000 here is Gore/Bradley defeating Bush or Forbes/Liddy Dole by a narrow margin, with Republican control of Congress expanding by five to ten seats.

Not that any of this matters much, since the left and right in the American spectrum are defined merely as the extremes of acceptable dinner conversation among the moneyed class while waiting for Carlos to decant the chiante.

Until you and I and the rest of the American public begin doing the real work of democracy, and take it on ourselves to force a change in the way campaigns are financed, the election will remain largely a sideshow, a bait-and-switch carnival game creating the illusion of actual democracy while retaining little of its practical meaning.

Or at least ninety-six percent of it is.

Speaking of the money being raised...Recognize these names?

Richard and Helen DeVos
Peter Buttenwieser
Bernard and Irene Schwartz
Carl and Edyth Lindner
John Childs
S. Daniel Abraham
Alan Solomont and Susan Lewis
Julian and Josephine Robertson
Orin Kramer
David and Sylvia Steiner

What do these people have in common?

Nope, they're not the Kenneth Starr grand jury.

They're not the Washington Redskins' starting defense, either, although their win-loss record would be pretty much the same.

They're not even the complete list of people who paid eight bucks for that Vanessa Williams dance movie, although that's the most believable guess of the three.

According to data compiled by the non-partisan Center for Responsive Politics, these are the leading financial contributors to the current election cycle. You want to know how politicians choose their positions? Just ask somebody who owns one.

Take Richard and Helen DeVos, this year's champions. They're hyperconservative Amway moguls, essentially a Taliban faction with matching bathroom soaps. They give lots of money to the pro-lifers—but then *of course* a multi-level marketing scheme like Amway would support a population explosion.

Or take Bernie Schwartz, number three on the list. Bernie runs the Loral corporation and gave over a million bucks to the Democrats. So Bernie got a birthday party in the White House, and Clinton lets Loral launch satellites in China. Coincidence, of course.

Or take S. Daniel Abraham, number six on the charts. He was brilliant as Salieri opposite Tom Hulce, and if you look really close, he's one of the grapes in one of the old live-action Fruit Of The Loom ads.

Oh, wait. That was F. Murray Abraham. Wrong guy.

Sorry.

See? An informed electorate is our only hope.

And election results follow fundraising, as surely as swallows return to Capistrano and unwatchable sitcoms return to the WB. Which means this stuff is worth knowing.

You can find the lowdown on the 400 biggest bankrolls currently filling the beltway moneybelt at *Mother Jones* magazine's website, www.motherjones.com.

Ask around. If anyone you know thinks Orin Kramer lived next door to Seinfeld, remember: their vote counts as much as yours does.

As to how all that money gets spent, and why the media doesn't do a better job of reporting the elections as the enormous auction they truly are:

Bill Clinton announced a while back that the corruption caused by private campaign financing can be solved by requiring broad-casters to provide free TV time to candidates. The President sug-gested that such a measure would help "free our democracy from the grip of big money."

What he didn't add is that a grip, applied two ways, is called a handshake.

Just hours after making the proposal, Clinton attended a $25,000-a-plate swordfish dinner in the Crystal Ballroom of the Carlton Hotel. In exchange for some grins with the guests and a couple of Kodak moments, Clinton raised over half-a-million-dollars—*ninety percent* of which would have been illegal under the man's own recommendations.

Brazen? It gets better. As the speculators and land sharks savored their candied chestnut ice cream, Clinton actually rose up and speechified about the need for reform, saying that "there is much more to do." Besides look in the mirror, apparently.

We're talking serious brass. I'm surprised the TV mics don't pick up the rhythmic clanking when the President jogs.

Why the lip service? Needing to happyface the ongoing revelations about White House fundraising—go to the side door, small bills only, ask for Lenny—Clinton cleverly tried to lower the heat by posing as a do-gooder, advocating a populist reform that he knows has zero chance of happening in the near-term.

Make no mistake, the free TV proposal *would* help, and it's entirely doable, at least hypothetically. (The mythical "free market" doesn't apply here, since the broadcast industry wouldn't even exist without goverment-protected monopolies over individual frequencies.)

Not that such a mandate is likely. You're asking for concerted altruism from a bunch of silk-suited politicians and TV execs. You might as well ask a humming swarm of locusts to play "Kum By Yah."

See, the Democrats want to keep the White House in 2000, which means Al Gore is about to eat more seafood dinners than Moby Dick. As will the various Great Whites of the GOP.

And once that first fifty million or so is burning a pocket hole, where do you think Al's gonna blow it? As you've probably realized, the ultimate recipient of much of the money spent in political campaigns is the media itself.

Next election season, go visit a TV station and sit in the lobby for an hour or two. You'll see an amazingly constant stream of opposing campaign staffers buying time and dropping off their latest attack ads and rebuttals. As you'd imagine, the more panicky the one-upmanship gets, the calmer the station beancounters become. It's like watching a poker game where no matter who raises the bet, the casino gets to keep every chip.

In turn, the media reinvests a big chunk of cash into candidates who favor proposals to make the Murdochs and Perelmans even richer. Clinton himself was financed in '96 in large part by Time-Warner, which, you'll notice, was the one media company Bob Dole consistently singled out for verbal abuse.

You think Clinton and Gore are gonna turn their backs on that cash by pushing the FCC to mandate free ad time? Sure, and Chevy Chase is just in a creative lull.

Predictably, the National Association of Broadcasters doesn't care for the idea of: a) giving away what they can sell, and b) losing the influence the ad money buys. So they're ready to start using their government-granted monopolies to synonymize private financing of TV ads, "free speech" (for those who can afford it), and the American flag until we're all half-convinced that Paul Revere brought coaxial cable to Concord and the Boston Tea Party was hosted by Carmen Electra.

Free TV for candidates simply can't fly if the media won't give it air.

There's only one real long-term solution—a public campaign financing system. Getting it will require citizen activism of a Civil Rights scale.

Which sounds like a big deal, but it's not asking much. We've no right to expect a healthy democracy until we behave like we actually have one.

Special Section on Newt Gingrich, Bob Dole, and $300,000

May 1997

In accepting $300,000 from Bob Dole to pay off his ethics fine in April, Newt Gingrich claims he took the high ground.

If enough folks examine the deal closely, he may have to head for the hills.

House rules only allow loans on terms "generally available to the public." That includes me, so I called five banks and asked for $300K unsecured at ten percent with no payments for eight years. They thought I was nuts. When I profiled Newt's income and net worth, all five still said no chance. (The best I found for him was only $25K, monthly payments, ten years, 13.9 percent.)

On its face, this deal was a bigger con than *Speed 2*.

Loans to Congressmen must also come from a financial institution—which Bob Dole isn't, although he's older than most—unless originating from a friend with no interest in buying influence.

That explains why both Dole and Gingrich, who notoriously don't like each other, took such pains to proclaim themselves "close personal friends" in various statements. Maybe that's their Ethics Committee loophole.

OK, so Dole and Gingrich are pals. Just like Tiger Woods and Fuzzy Zoeller. But does Bob Dole really have no interest in buying influence?

Dole's new day gig is "special counsel" for Verner, Liipfert, one of the biggest and most active lobbying firms in Washington.

In February 1997, the five tobacco monsters—Philip Morris, RJR, Brown & Williamson, UST, and Loews—retained Verner, Liipfert to lobby Congress.

The cancer kings were in major trouble: fifteen class action suits, twenty-three states suing for billions in Medicaid expenses, and then teeny Liggett fessing up that cigarettes are really, really bad.

However, Liggett also showed the bad guys a way out: admitting guilt and paying a fine, in exchange for immunity from future liability.

Since potential lawsuits might run over a trillion dollars, the barons of broadleaf need immunity so badly that they're willing to put their ads, their trademarks, $300 billion in fines, and FDA status as a drug on the bargaining table.

On April 3, after weeks of organizing, backroom negotiations began. The first meeting included four Attorneys General, two stogie moguls, a bunch of trial lawyers—and Verner, Liipfert.

Info on the meetings is scarce. However, any agreement they reach will have to be voted on by Congress.

That puts Mr. Speaker at the head of the tobacco lobby's kiss-up list. And he badly needs $300,000.

Gee, what to do, what to do…?

BACKGROUND

Dole and tobacco go way back. Four of the five tobacconists who hired Verner, Liipfert were among the top ten Republican donors during Dole's run at the White House; Philip Morris led all scorers with $2.5 million. Coincidentally, Dole opposed FDA actions to curb tobacco sales and marketing, grandstanded an anti-drug pose while not mentioning that cigarettes kill twenty-five times more Americans than all illegal narcotics combined, and even questioned tobacco's addictive qualities on national TV.

RETURN TO STORY

Who thought up the loan? "Dole just came up with it himself," said the Associated Press, quoting Charles Black, an "adviser to Dole" who did most of the talking. A curious spinmeister: Charles Black is a lobbyist whose biggest account last year was Philip Morris.

When did the loan idea originate? Dole's spokeswoman termed it "last minute" and "completely unexpected." But most GOP sources say Dole first broached the loan with Scott Reed, an actual friend of Newt, sometime near the first of April—just as tobacco liability talks began. Reed spoke to another go-between, and then Gingrich. (This is how "close, personal friends" usually talk.)

When did Newt accept the loan? His people pinpoint the evening of the 16th—apparently trophy wife Marianne gave the pants-wearing thumbs-up—but Newt's signature is on an agreement dated the 15th. Reed contacted Gingrich at least a week earlier. No one is being very specific about dates. It's not clear when Newt verbally agreed, but Dole wouldn't have called on the 15th if Newt hadn't already expressed interest. That was the whole point of sending Reed as an errand boy.

We do know that on April 9th, Verner, Liipfert hired Bob Dole.

The non-partisan National Journal's *CongressDaily* reports that Dole received a signing bonus of—coincidentally enough—$300,000. (Their source is a partner at Verner, Liipfert.)

That's just how much Dole fronted Gingrich six days later.

Curious? The major papers aren't. The Ethics Committee didn't care; the chairman was Utah's James Hansen, a conservative Republican. Slam dunk.

Dole denies that Verner, Liipfert had knowledge of the Gingrich loan; reportedly, most folks at the firm were embarrassed by the appearance of impropriety.

You can see why:

Verner, Liipfert works for tobacco. So does Dole, who now also works for Verner, Liipfert. Verner, Liipfert wants liability limits passed. During tobacco negotiations, Dole offers Newt a bailout. Verner, Liipfert gives Dole $300K. Dole puts $300K in Newt's hand six days later.

The high ground smells a lot like a tobacco field.

P.S.—Liddy Dole has recently given Red Cross jobs to several of hubby Dole's campaign advisors. Either she's running for President, or there's a sudden medical demand for Spin Doctors. Let's see if Newt throws his full weight behind Liddy shortly after next year's mid-term elections.

December 1997

In a column written over six months ago, I predicted ("The Dole/Gingrich Bailout," May 1, 1997) that Elizabeth Dole would run for President in 2000.

Why? Because Bob Dole has never made a habit of giving a political favor without collecting something in return. And in accepting $300,000 from tobacco lobbying firm Verner, Liipfert and forwarding a notably similar sum to Gingrich only six days later, Dole took a tremendous (and so far successful) risk that both his and the GOP's mythical high ground on shady campaign fundraising might be lost for good.

What might Dole want from Gingrich in return for saving Newt's career? Bob Dole's own political career is over. The only imaginable incentive is Gingrich's support in rallying the conservative wing of the GOP to Liddy's cause.

Wild speculation? Nope. Check out Liddy's personal staff: a bunch of Bob's campaign organizers were hired by the Mrs. over at the Red Cross. There are exactly two possible reasons for this. Either:

a) there was a sudden need for Republican fundraisers in Third World war zones, or

b) Liddy was doing groundwork for her own run at the White House.

Early money is key in national campaigns, because election-year contributors rarely fork over for a candidate who's already behind. That's why Dan Quayle began his campaign for 2000 before '96 had even ended. That's why Bob Kasich, Lamar Alexander, Steve Forbes, and the rest of the whiteshirts are already visiting Iowa and New Hampshire.

And that's why, three years before the 2000 elections, Bob Dole was already stumping for Liddy.

Just as *Meet The Press* received major media attention for its 50th anniversary, Bob Dole went on the show and pointedly stated that the Republican Party should consider putting a woman on the ticket in 2000. Why? Dole gave two reasons: a) to reduce the "gender gap," wherein women vote by large margins for Democratic candidates, and b) because "I've still got one chance to get there— if Elizabeth runs."

Dole also added, unsurprisingly, "I think she is certainly qualified."

Oh, really?

Elizabeth Dole was Secretary of Labor for a while, Secretary of Transportation another time, and currently runs the American Red Cross. She also did a nice impression of Oprah at the convention in San Diego.

Swell.

Now remember that Liddy has never stood as a candidate for public office, much less actually raised campaign funds or won an election.

Never mind the guys; Elizabeth Dole isn't even the GOP's best-qualified *woman*. Off the top of my head, New Jersey Governor Christine Todd Whitman has been a prominent and consistent electoral winner, as have Maine Senators Susan Collins and Olympia Snowe. There's also Senator Kay Bailey Hutchison (R-Texas), former Labor Secretary and Congresswoman Lynne Cheney (R-Illinois), and pothead-turned-anti-drug-Congresswoman-turned-CBS-talking-head Susan Molinari (R-New York).

Aw heck, even Rep. Helen Chenoweth (Lunatic-Idaho), who spouts militia-inspired nonsense about black helicopters, UN internment camps, and the environmental movement as a plot to enslave Americans, has won more actual elections than Elizabeth Dole.

Obviously, if Liddy wasn't married to Bob, there's not much chance she'd be in the race.

Which means Liddy is an intelligent, articulate, telegenic woman whose main qualification for the White House is that she occasionally sleeps with a famous politician.

If that's political progress for women, Bob Dole and the GOP still have a lot to learn.

This column also predicted in May that Newt would support Liddy's campaign sometime after the 1998 mid-term elections, when the memory of the tobacco payoff will presumably have faded.

That's still a year away. Let's keep an eye on Newt and enjoy the show.

January 1999

In May 1997, my column pointed out the odd coincidence between the $300,000 Bob Dole fronted to bail Newt Gingrich's more photogenic end out of his Ethics Committee penalty for lying, and the $300,000 Dole received a few days earlier as a signing bonus to begin working for the tobacco lobby.

Since the only conceivable motivation for Dole's entering such a deal would be political advantage, this space predicted more than a year ago that Liddy Dole would definitely seek the presidency in 2000, and that Newt Gingrich would not. Instead, Newt would defer and support Liddy.

So. Am I nuts, or was the loan from Dole part of a deal to buy Gingrich's patronage? And did Dole, by fronting for them, buy Gingrich's support for Liddy?

Time cut to the present.

Liddy's running.

Newt's not.

(Two predictions down, two to go.)

Instead, Newt's setting up Gingrich Enterprises, a consulting firm to lobby on (get this) *health* issues, presumably including tobacco. Newt's also about to start a speaking tour at $50,000 a pop.

Newt's also setting up a new PAC, the Friends of Newt Gingrich Political Action Committee. So obviously he'll be raising money for *somebody* in 2000.

How long will it be before Newt throws his girth behind Liddy? I'll follow the saga at www.bobharris.com.

Let's also watch and see if Newt starts doing a bunch of speeches for tobacco growers and the like. Let's see how much FNGPAC (which I suggest we begin pronouncing as "Fang-Pac") money winds up in Liddy's coffers.

Just as a coincidence, of course.

Chapter Nine

We Pull Their Lever, They Yank Our Chain

Seems like the only thing Congress did in 1998 was frown about oral sex and denounce each other. That's because in 1998 that *was* all they did. But only because nobody believes in witches anymore. Then they'd have been really busy.

Surprisingly, however, they actually passed a federal budget. How they accomplished this when ten minutes of Monica Lewinsky's preteen years still haven't been broadcast to Fiji we'll never know. But somehow they managed.

You remember this Congress was elected largely on a platform of streamlining government and eliminating waste, right? Unfortunately, the 1998 budget included literally hundreds of millions of dollars for things that are, to put it gently, psychotic.

A few examples:

$700,000 of your money is building a pedestrian overpass in a town with a population of 306.

$15,000,000 of your money is renovating a gravel airstrip in a town with a population of 451. (Yes, I said fifteen *million*. It's in Alaska. There's oil.)

One million dollars is even going to something called the Thad Cochran National Warmwater Aquaculture Center. Which is at Mississippi State University. Where they grow catfish.

And who is Thad Cochran, you ask? Thad Cochran is:

> a Senator from Mississippi
>
> who sits on the Appropriations Committee
>
> that approved the funding for
>
> the Thad Cochran National Warmwater Aquaculture Center at Mississippi State.

Oh. Of course.

How did this happen? Simple: by the time all the pork was added on, the final budget was over four *thousand* pages long.

Few of the Congressmen who signed it even read the whole thing.

No wonder there's so little money budgeted for education. Nobody in Washington is willing to do their homework.

I speak at colleges constantly, and I *swear* to you that more than half the time, the student introducing me is barely able to read my printed introduction.

I get a little tired of performing before a roomful of people who think David Bowie was killed at the Alamo.

Especially when we all know he really died in front of Tin Machine.

But anyway.

It turns out that precious little educational innovation is actually happening. Instead, most of the discretionary money in the national education budget is getting diverted into pork-barrel local stuff that serves only the interests of a few well-connected contributors or the members of one Senator's district.

In the last year, you and I have had the privilege of helping to pay for:

> the Paul Simon Public Policy Institute
> in Carbondale, Illinois, and
>
> the Robert J. Dole Institute for Public Service
> in Lawrence, Kansas,

neither of which is going to change the way kids are taught to read in the 99.96 percent of America not located in these two throbbing metropoles.

We've also paid hundreds of thousands of dollars to assemble an oral history of labor unions in Iowa, the home state of Senator Tom Harkin, a ranking Democrat on the Appropriations Committee, and about ten million for an exhibit on the Constitution in

Philadelphia, hometown of Senator Arlen Specter, the ranking Republican.

So what do we do about it? Educate ourselves, first off.

Which, if we don't do anything about it, is exactly what we'll all wind up doing anyway.

My Grandpa was a coal miner until one day he landed a better gig as a dairy farmer. That's a big step up—from working in a hole and suffocating, to living in fresh air and sunshine. It's like getting fired as a TV writer.

Actually, Grandpa's new gig was even better than that: Grandpa eventually became one of those dairy farmers the government pays *not* to produce milk. Pretty good gig. I don't produce milk myself, either, but I've never figured out how to get paid for it.

Apparently you have to have the actual capacity to do something before you can get wildly overpaid not to. Which explains the New York Knicks' payroll, but that's another topic.

Supposedly, subsidies like Grandpa's maintain "price stability" for various commodities. That's the excuse, anyway. Make the same argument about human labor, all of a sudden you're a raving socialist. But somehow when the handouts go to their major contributors, most Congressmen turn left more predictably than the pace car at the Indy 500.

Sometimes, however, the subsidies become completely ridiculous. This is actually in the current budget: in an effort to alleviate a glut of physicians—you see them on the curb all the time with little signs: "Will Overmedicate For Food"—the government is going to pay America's teaching hospitals hundreds of millions of dollars *not* to train doctors.

See, residency training is currently subsidized with Medicare money, and the budget says that hospitals which downsize keep getting more money for up to five years as an incentive. So we'll spring for a gigabuck or so and get *less* people able to treat illness in return.

I guess we get the government we deserve. I mean, obviously, we're paying all this tax money every year *not* to have rational leadership.

GOP Congressman Bill Archer came up with a bold plan to make it harder for the IRS to barge into your house, take your stuff, and ruin your life.

Sounds good. So far.

Archer says—and most folks agree—that in disputed cases the burden of proof should lie with the IRS, instead of the taxpayer.

Damn straight. So far.

As things stand, if some IRS data coolie blows a decimal point and his Apple IIe decides you owe enough cash to upgrade his whole division to the Macintosh Plus, you're the one that has to prove *him* wrong. Meanwhile, you're running up penalties and interest; fight long enough, and you'll face seizure and worse.

That's just plain wrong. So far, so good.

Naturally, Archer's idea became popular. Just as naturally, Bill Clinton initially sided with the IRS, changing his mind only after a long night of soul-searching and incoming focus group data.

(Clinton's opinion-mongering is now so reflexive he'd probably support his own defenestration if it meant a boost in the polls: "The people have spoken. The people want to hurl me through this window. And so, tonight, I say to all Americans: EEYAAAHHHHhhhthunk.")

There's just one problem: when, exactly, did Bill Archer and the GOP suddenly start caring about the Bill of Rights?

These are, after all, the same folks who would happily eliminate, among other things, the First Amendment in online communications, the Fourth and Fifth in alleged drug and terrorist cases, and the Sixth through Eighth in immigration and capital cases.

And now, suddenly, they care about the Constitution?

Sure, the Archer plan might keep the IRS from knocking down your door—but what are you supposed to do about a surprise visit from the DEA, the INS, the BATF, the FBI, or the producers of *Cops*? Tough luck, Orange Jumpsuit Boy.

Don't get me wrong: shifting the burden of proof from citizens onto the IRS is long overdue. I've been audited myself. Yowch. I'll never forget the first time I got an official letter gently ordering me to present myself downtown and hand over the paper trail of my entire life. I bloody near fainted. (Of course, when a hungry animal has you in its jaws, it's only natural to play dead.) So I feel your pain.

But remember how our political system works: follow the money. Bill Archer is the Congressman from Houston, which means he inevitably represents the interests of a bunch of oil and aerospace firms who: a) like paying taxes even less than you do, and b) have lawyers who can string together enough loopholes to knit a Persian rug.

Is it possible *that's* who this new proposal is really for? You betcha.

Bill Archer's the same guy who so recently pushed to abolish the Alternative Minimum Tax (AMT). Remember hearing about Fortune 500 companies who avoided paying even a dime to Uncle Sam? The AMT was created in 1986 precisely to force the big boys to pay their fair share.

Jump cut to two years ago: it was Archer leading the backroom effort to sneak a repeal of the AMT into law—thereby moving almost $10 billion a year out of the Treasury and into the Forbes 400.

So much for balanced budgets...

By the way, 10 gig is roughly the same budget chunk the government *couldn't* afford for Aid to Families With Dependent Children. Evidently, giving money to the rich is good; giving money to the poor is bad.

So listen closely. Archer's fanfare for the common man is really just the same corporate brass line given a catchy pop motif. Sure, you and I might indeed retain relative handfuls of cash and privacy—while the biggest tax deadbeats in America make off with entire bankloads.

Predictably, the major papers hailed Archer without mentioning his well-documented long-term agenda. Apparently nobody in the mainstream has a memory extending back to 1995.

Bill Bradley isn't the only basketball player who understands Washington.

Let's back up. I'm from Ohio, where we have the glorious Cleveland Cavaliers, a team so consistently lame that in almost thirty years, they've never once gotten even close to a championship. In fact, the one year they managed to remain in the semifinals for seven whole games before finally losing—the year they stank least—is actually called the "Miracle of Richfield."

(Richfield, by the way, is the rural suburb twenty miles out of town where they built the old arena. Which is how I always figured the place got its name: they put the building in a field, they got rich, Richfield.)

The Cavs did have a couple of good years in the mid-'80s, however. They had Brad Daugherty, who could pass really well for a center; Larry Nance, who could pass really well for a forward; and Mark Price, one of the best passing guards in the league. It's too bad they didn't have anyone who could actually shoot the ball, or they would have been something to see.

Those Cavs lost a lot of games to the Detroit Pistons, who had a bunch of guys who *could* shoot the ball, and a center named Bill Laimbeer who would beat you up if you tried to stop them.

Laimbeer used to play for the Cavs a long time ago, but he was really lousy then, probably because he hadn't yet discovered beating people up. Once he got to Detroit, apparently he began beating people up to fit into the local culture, liked the way it felt, and stayed with it until he got good.

Well, the fine folks of Detroit haven't forgotten Bill Laimbeer. In fact, they've been trying to get him to run for Congress, where apparently they think a lot of people need beating up. Damn straight.

And y'know what? He won't do it.

Why? Because, he says, "politics is too ugly a sport…and getting worse every day."

You want proof things are bad in Washington? *Bill Laimbeer* won't go there. A guy who beat people up for a living thinks it's "too ugly."

Sorry, Detroit. But don't give up hope: Dennis Rodman is still available.

The state of Oregon is an extremely pleasant place. You don't hear much about it, largely because lots of people who go there simply never leave. The scenery is gorgeous, the cities are clean, and most of the really scary people have already moved to Idaho.

There's another reason why some Oregon visitors, many from as far away as Florida or New England, never leave:

Legalized doctor-assisted suicide.

This figures: the only place you can legally kill yourself is the last place you'd ever want to.

Anyway, neighboring Washington also considered legalizing assisted suicide. Not surprising: in a state with thousands of Microsoft employees, when it comes to pressing the cosmic Escape key, they probably can't help but go after market share.

However, some Washingtonians think physician-assisted suicide is a bad idea—apparently, such things are best left to amateurs—so they published a scary handbill claiming that if the measure passed, "your eye doctor could kill you."

Well, heck, your eye doctor can kill you right now.

So can a proctologist, for that matter.

Me, I'm taking the eye doctor.

What they meant was: your eye doctor could kill you *legally*.

Still, that's not what the bill was really about, so the pro-legal-suicide folks filed a complaint under a Washington law that says lying in political campaigns is a crime.

Of course, if anyone paid much attention to a law against political lying, they'd probably have to just put locks on the legislature door and be done with it.

Anyhow, the law about lying went all the way to the state Supreme Court, which threw it out—ruling that the First Amendment even applies to a calculated lie.

Honest.

Which means: next year, when Spokane Republicans accuse Clinton of sleeping with a lemur, and Seattle Democrats respond that Tom DeLay is an alien space robot controlled by the tobacco lobby, it's all part of the big fun stew we call democracy.

Which would be really depressing. But still nothing to move to Oregon over.

Here's at least one novel way to breathe life into politics: vote for the dead.

The last Congress didn't accomplish much beyond debating the meaning to our Republic of a stain on a dress much the same way tribesmen in New Guinea debate the meaning of bird droppings to their future chieftains.

The main difference here is that our droppings come directly *from* our chief. But anyway.

Given how stiff this Congress has been, I've often wondered whether any less would get done if they actually were no longer with us. Maybe Congress would get just as much accomplished even if they all just quietly passed on the House floor one day like John Quincy Adams.

Except for Strom Thurmond, of course, since he's immortal and cannot be killed. In fact, he personally knew John Quincy Adams. I think I actually saw Senator Thurmond on a *Highlander* episode once. But anyway.

Y'know, dead Senators don't take PAC money. Maybe it wouldn't be any worse.

At least that seems to be what they're saying in Oklahoma, where Senate candidate Jacquelyn Ledgerwood—who died more than six weeks beforehand—*still* got more than twenty percent of the vote in the 1998 Democratic primary. She didn't win, but she did prevent anybody else from getting a majority, so there had to be a runoff.

While a lot of voters didn't know she was dead, according to exit polls, lots of them *did*, and voted for her anyway. So she got over 50,000 votes, enough to finish second out of four.

You gotta feel for the guys in third and fourth. Talk about rejection: you spend all that time and money and get your butt kicked by somebody who doesn't even have a pulse.

It's probably how Donald Trump felt when he divorced Ivana. Anyhow.

And it gets better. Oklahoma law dictated that Miz Ledgerwood's name appeared on the ballot for the runoff.

Which meant that Oklahoma voters had possibly the clearest-cut choice in American history: live guy vs. dead woman, going head to head for the chance to lead the state into the next century.

Unfortunately, Oklahoma voters chose a live guy, so we'll never know how far this could have gone.

The winner entered the general election against incumbent GOP Senator Don Nickles. Who is not dead, and has no plans to die at the current time.

Although if Miz Ledgerwood had pulled off an upset, he might have had to reconsider his platform.

Part IV

―――――

$

Chapter Ten

This Chapter Heading for Rent

I grew up watching the Cleveland Browns play football in old Municipal Stadium.

You couldn't have asked for a lamer name for a ballpark. You might as well have called it Ordinary Field or Generic Arena. But so what? We were there as fans, not as members of a consumer market. Municipal was just fine.

There were lots of places like that. Metropolitan in Minneapolis. County stadiums in Milwaukee and Atlanta. Memorials in Baltimore, Philadelphia, and Buffalo. Other titles were often either beautifully descriptive—Mile High, Three Rivers, Fenway—or simplest of all, named for the team: Yankee, Tiger, Dodger.

Well, old Municipal Stadium is gone, and so is any chance we'll ever see a name like that again. The Oakland Raiders' place is now called the UMAX Coliseum. Riverfront is now Cinergi Field. Candlestick? 3COM Park.

It's happening in every sport these days. Home or away, if the Bulls tip-off with the Suns, the arena's named for an airline; if the Bruins skate against the Flyers, it's a bank; and if the Rockies and Cardinals play a doubleheader, someone's selling beer.

I can't be the only one who's getting fed up with having every square inch of American life sold for ad space. We lose something when we surrender Joe Louis for Alltel, PacBell, or Qualcomm. I'll take RFK over RCA, TWA, or ARCO any day.

OK, I know, it's a free country. There's nothing stopping you from turning the tables. Maybe you can even sweet-talk some Internet start-up into tattooing their website address on your forehead.

And, hey, there's always money to be made by auctioning off the naming rights to our children. "This one, the teenager, is Commodore—he's our oldest—and these are the twins, Yahoo and Java."

Now that I mention it, how long do you think it'll be until somebody actually does that?

One notch above fast food joints are those nicer, franchised sit-down restaurants, invariably bedubbed with skin-crawlingly cutesy names that would make an Osmond choke:

T.J. McCookieCutter's

Cap'n Happy's Chuckle Bucket

Ol' Mama Stifleluvin's Biskitz'n'Ribz

B.M. Misspeller's Crapulous Disgorge-O-Mat

and so on.

You know the drill: wood and brass fixtures, baseball pennants and license plates on the walls, and a menu with little hearts next to the four entrees out of 110 that won't cause you to leave a ventricle as a tip.

A while back, the folks at a college I performed at took me to one of these places. The food was actually pretty good, but even the washroom was fixed to the gills with cloying, saccharine photos of kids with catcher's mitts, dogs licking kittens, and absurdly fat people scratching themselves.

This was all a little more visual input than I needed right that minute.

So two nights later and two states over, another college took me to another unit of the same chain. Sure enough: wood and brass, baseball pennants, little hearts...

If you've seen the old TV series *The Prisoner*, somewhere in the distance you could almost hear a bald guy with goggles murmuring, "begin program."

And then I used the washroom.

To my horror, it was *completely identical* to the one 200 miles away: Dogs. Kids. Fat scratch fever. Right down to the molecule.

Which means some high-paid consultant has actually focus-grouped, market-researched, and maximized the profit margin on my relieving experience.

It's more than just a bathroom—it's a highly tested waste facility of FUN!

AIEEE!!!

Please, corporate America.

For the love of God.

Stop trying to please me 24/7. Stop trying to optimize me. Not everyone is comfortable on the other side of your one-way glass.

Allow us just the tiniest respite, just one brief moment of contemplation, just a single room in the world where we can escape your never-ending influence.

In short: Let my people *go*.

Televised golf tournaments are the reason that Hell is wired for cable: seventy-two channels, nothing but golf, welcome to Hell, here's your remote.

I just can't seem to fully appreciate the subtlety of watching flabby millionaires whacking and walking and walking and whacking for four non-stop hours of fun, punctuated with commercials for financial services I'll never need unless I accidentally marry a Forbes.

My friends who actually enjoy such things insisted I should watch a major tournament all the way through sometime, so I'd *really understand*. OK, I did, and I do. I watched the Masters last year, and I'll admit I learned a lot.

I learned that, just like everywhere else in the world, almost anything remotely near your visual field—from the side of a golf bag to a hand towel to the back of a player's glove—is becoming ad space.

I learned that some of the players even sell ads on their feet and pant legs, so that when the camera zooms in during a putt, the corporate logo fills the screen.

And I learned that, at least among the well-off who can afford the stuff the advertisers are selling, a frightening value system prevails.

The Traveler's Insurance people, who are branching out into a broader range of financial schemes, repeated a series of ads all weekend in which various objects were creatively captioned to help us perceive them anew.

I'm quoting here:

"This is not a baseball game; this is a steady cash flow…"

"This is not a church; this is a site on the World Wide Web…"

"This is not a four-year-old; this is 3.4 million dollars in lifetime income…"

Whoa.

I thought at first the ads were some sort of self-parody.

After seeing them a dozen times, I'm convinced they're not. Travelers is now a financial services company seriously trying to redefine themselves as innovative players on the global stage. If you aren't supposed to perceive the remapping of religion, tradition, and simple humanity into dollar signs as something creative and cool, then you wouldn't be expected to think the same of the redesign of the company itself.

So Travelers is actually bragging about their ability to see a four-year-old child in purely financial terms.

Y'know, I'd worry for those people's souls, but then again, there's no reason to.

Where they're going, at least they'll enjoy the cable TV.

Chapter Eleven

Greed,

or The 9 Steps to the 7 Habits of the 3 People Who Own Every Freaking Thing on Earth

The degree to which some Americans will go to set themselves apart and above others dismays and amazes me.

I've only flown First Class once in my life, and that was an accident when the airline overbooked. For the life of me, I've never understood the attraction of sitting in the Old Fat White Guy section. You arrive at the exact same time as everybody else, you get real silverware but it's still airline food, and the stewardesses are still just pretending they don't hate you. Why would you pay twice as much just to get to sit in a big chair? Either you have a really enormous ass, or God's trying to imply you have way too much money.

Same thing with a luxury box at a ballgame. Oooee, you've got a kitchen and a reclining chair and a television. Congratulations, Stephen Hawking, I've got the same thing at home, and I don't pay twelve bucks to park.

And now, in selected test cities, three big movie theatre chains are offering VIP seating. You get a private little booth to sit in, a private bathroom, and even a concierge to hold your hand while you go there.

Yick.

What's next, valet parking at the bowling alley?

Look, if you want, you can spend a hundred dollars a seat to see Keanu Reeves and Demi Moore star in a Kevin Costner film written by Joe Eszterhas.

The VIP booth still won't have an eject button.

Twenty years ago when I was a kid, I could get a bleacher seat at a Cleveland Indians game for—this is true—fifty cents.

Now granted, that was to watch the Indians, who were to quality baseball what Trent Lott is to raw sexual intensity. And the bleacher seats were almost 100 feet behind the center field fence, so far from home plate that no one ever once hit a ball that far in the sixty years they played baseball there.

(In fact, they didn't even build the stadium for baseball per se. It was built for, among other things, Cleveland's bid for the 1936 Olympics. Apparently, the Olympic committee took one look around and said, gee, Cleveland's nice, thanks, but we're more comfortable in Nazi Germany.)

When I was a kid, the best seat behind home plate was only four bucks. On a paper route, I could afford four box seats a week if I wanted.

This just in: the New York Mets are paying pitcher Hideo Nomo, who only won them four more games last year than I did, five million dollars. They gave his catcher, Mike Piazza, enough money to buy the Montreal Expos.

Somebody's gotta pay for these sins. So guess how much some seats behind home plate are gonna cost? A hundred fifty bucks.

One of these days the only people who can afford to see a game will be the players themselves.

Thanks to a new designer label, the Lizard Women of Beverly Hills might no longer adorn their scaly hides in so much animal fur.

If you're not sure what I mean because your neighborhood isn't afflicted with rampaging Lizard Women, stay with me. I had never seen one myself until the recording of my radio commentaries was moved to a fancy studio just one block away from Rodeo Drive, Ground Zero when they finally drop the Opulence Bomb.

It still feels a little weird to spew forth my progressive babble from a studio fit for the Sultan of Brunei. I'd even worry about selling out, except full-body immersion in the excesses surrounding my lovely new workplace is very possibly making me even more radical.

It's one thing to read statistics about the concentration of wealth. It's quite another to drive a girlfriend to a job interview at an L.A. public school which doubles as an enormous ad hoc graffiti mural, and then later go to work just fifty yards from an art gallery where similar, less-inspired abstracts sell for more than the price of the school itself.

What a bizarre world I have entered.

Where I'm from in Ohio, aging is simple: Your body gradually becomes triangular, *Diagnosis Murder* reruns suddenly become interesting, and then one fine morning you wake up in a silk jogging suit. Shortly thereafter they close the lid. Aging is considered inevitable, and it's accepted with dignity, grace, and black socks with shorts.

In Beverly Hills, however, aging is merely the process of surgically removing ever-larger pieces of your own face. This is the only place in the world where "paper or plastic" refers to the texture of your current skin. Half of these women have their faces pulled so tight they can't even blink because their eyelids are holding their ears on.

(Cue *Mutual of Omaha's Wild Kingdom* theme music.)

These, my friends, are the Lizard Women of Beverly Hills. And when the days get short, they commonly wrap themselves in animal furs to keep their cold-blooded bodies warm through the arctic L.A. winter.

But maybe not for long. Animal-rights people here have pushed a special election to decide whether or not new fur coats should carry the following tag:

WARNING—this product is made from animals that may have been killed by electrocution, gassing, neck breaking, poisoning, clubbing, stomping, or drowning.

Eek.

Subtlety isn't exactly a high art with the animal-rights people.

Or is it? Notice there's nothing in there about being skinned alive.

That's understandable.

For a lot of Lizard Women, skinning alive might just be a little too close to home.

You've dealt with insurance companies. These people have as much kindness toward their fellow man as Don King, only without the cool hair.

A few months ago, an eighty-one-year-old woman named Gertie Witherspoon was run over on a Missouri highway by a big rig hauling grain.

Shortly thereafter, the late Miz Witherspoon's daughter received notice that the truck's insurance company was suing *her*—for her mother's negligence at being in the middle of the street. The Great Western Casualty Company actually came after the dead grandmother's daughter to get $2800 to cover the cost of repairing the dents in the front of the truck that killed her.

How rude of your mother, they said, to crush herself like a bug and mess up the chrome on our truck's front grillwork. Shame on you, they said.

Shame on them.

Fortunately, they had enough shame that they withdrew their claim for damages.

Their claim to belong to the human race they're still maintaining. For now.

So Richard Branson's big balloon came crashing down. Whoopty freaking do.

Am I the only one who couldn't care less about this story?

Unless you live in a cave or toil in Martha Stewart's slave labor doily mines, you remember hearing hour-by-hour updates of the ongoing travails of Richard Branson, the Virgin CEO. Not to be confused with Elizabeth I, the Virgin Queen. Although I bet there are a lot of virgin CEOs out there, which would explain why they need to run the world so bad, but anyway.

So Richard Branson, who has enough money that after dinner in a fancy restaurant he once left an NBA power forward as a tip, teamed up with a bazillionaire Chicago stock options broker and some Swedish guy (who is apparently the one doing most of the actual work) to try to fly all the way around the world on nothing but hot air, for which you usually have to be a member of the U.S. Senate.

Somehow I just can't root for a bunch of guys who can afford to dodge the ionosphere when most people I know can barely afford a Dodge Stratosphere.

They managed to make it from Morocco to the Pacific Ocean before gravity did its thing and they came plummeting back to Earth faster than Vanilla Ice. And everyone's reporting how this Branson guy lost a $300,000 bet which would have paid ten-to-one, and he would have given the three million to charity.

Nobody's saying anything about how maybe if he really cared about his charities, he might not have wasted a fortune on the Icarus Express trying to buy himself two lines in the Guinness book, but simply given the oodles to charity in the first place.

But what do I know? Branson's now tanning in the Caribbean, the options trader is skiing in the Rockies, and the Swedish guy is still back in the Pacific, cleaning up their mess.

Him, I can root for.

Defying all reason—like most of pop culture—the collective recovered memory (with all the accuracy that implies) of Diana Spencer has become something of a touchstone for the democratic impulse.

Diana's tragic end—coming when Death accidentally confused her with Ted Kennedy, who now gets to drift away gently in a canopy bed while spooning a Saudi prince—and even more tragic interspecies coupling with Charles have somehow converted the princess into a symbol of the common touch.

As usual, it approaches sacrilege to point out the obvious—in this case, that the Empress in fact had very New Clothes.

What you and I both remember is that in life, Diana's conspicuous appetite for travel, glamour, and fashion displayed the proletarian restraint of a Fabergé egg, causing the family treasury to slough off more Pounds than Rush Limbaugh on a Slim-Fast IV drip. Not that the royals are suddenly gonna show up hawking costume jewelry and silk jogging suits on QVC. Other than Fergie.

Which isn't to say Diana was any worse than most folks. Or better. She was just a chick. Precisely my point. They auctioned off $3,000,000.00 worth of her clothes and gave the money to charity. That's great. That Diana felt the need to wear $3,000,000.00 around town first, when the money was just as badly needed, isn't. Good and bad. Human. That's all I'm saying here. Don't hit me.

But thanks to a full week of elite media Two Minutes Grief, overshadowing even the passing of the actual Mother Teresa (whose relatively anonymous demise can only be attributed to an inability to wear Dior with panache), Diana's normal human desire not to see children nicknamed Skippy thanks to a landmine has somehow been received as an almost revolutionary level of compassion.

Obviously, many Britons intuitively expect their aristocracy to reside firmly in the pro-landmine, pro-maiming camp.

Egad.

Maybe that says something about the humanity of a system literally founded on privilege.

(At least the English know their leaders' dark sides better than we do. 135 nations have signed the Ottawa Mine Ban treaty, including Britain. The U.S., which has a full stockpile, has not. Surprised?)

So now, after years of the royals nosediving into deep muck faster than Valujet, the very legitimacy of regal authority is open to question, and constitutional monarchy itself just might face a shorter life expectancy than Robert Downey. So Britain's first family is trying to figure out how better to understand the common people.

Gee, maybe if they'd start sleeping with people they aren't related to. But what do I know.

The shake-up even extends to Britain's bicameral legislature, which includes:

a) the House of Commons, where Britain's leaders shout things about each other's ancestry, and

b) the House of Lords, where they have the paperwork to prove it.

Seats in the House of Lords have been passed by heredity among the gentry for almost as many centuries as insanity and venereal disease, but recently, the QE II broke her moorings and declared that birthright and wealth, by themselves, should not be sufficient to qualify for membership.

The irony that Grammy Windsor should be able to decree such a thing—purely because of her wealth and birthright—wasn't mentioned.

In turn, the assembly of ermine-and-scarlet-bedecked Lords broke from their traditional silence in the presence of the Queen, by—this is true—*emitting a series of audible growls*.

No report yet on how many Lords pawed the ground, snorted, and waved their forelegs in the air.

So let's hear it for the U.K., as they take this important (if almost entirely symbolic) step toward representative democracy.

And thank goodness we in the U.S. have no such hereditary, class-based claims on our leadership.

Whichever of America's three leading Presidential candidates wins in 2000—whether it's Al Gore (son of a Senator), George W. Bush (son of a President and grandson of a Senator), or Steve Forbes (son of one of the richest men on Earth)—we can be sure democracy has been served.

Chapter Twelve

Wall Street
Stocks, Bonds, and
Other Kinky Devices

As you know, we Americans are notoriously bad at math: two-thirds of us barely understand percentages, while the other three-fifths have trouble with fractions.

Ba-da-bum. Thank you. I'm here all week.

You see this inability on TV all the time—most often in financial news, where you commonly hear stuff like, "a good day on Wall Street: the Dow jumped nine points."

"Jumped?" nine points, when the Dow is at 9000, is one-tenth of one percent, or roughly twice the percentage of original jokes on *Suddenly Susan*. But particularly in local news coverage, you'll often hear the same chirpy tone whether it's nine points or ninety, whether the Dow is at 5000 or 10000.

The last time the market tanked bigtime—October 1997's Black Monday, when the Dow fell 550 points in one day—all the Armani-clad dental work started panicking, sounding less like expert commentators than a bunch of frightened astrologers: "The bull is on the wane! Perhaps the bear ascends! The moon is eating the sun!"

Rarely, if ever, have so many knowing so little about so much said so much of so little about something so small.

Let's put things in perspective.

That was the biggest one-day loss in stock market history, right?

Actually, no. In percentage terms, which is what matters, it wasn't even in the top ten. This wasn't Black Monday. Taupe, maybe.

And even if the fall *had* been the largest ever, the market would still have been roughly where it was during the Atlanta Olympics.

Were we all living in barrels back then? No? OK.

So big deal. The Dow Jones went down like Bill Clinton greeting Jiang Zemin. And maybe a bunch of yuppie IRAs give a little ground for a while. Whoopty.

Truth is, focusing so much attention on simple, seemingly objective indeces like the Nasdaq, Nikkei, Footsie, Bovespa, and Hüsker Dü (OK, that's actually a band I like), actually prevents everybody from confronting the crazed inequities those numbers so often camouflage.

Example: the paper losses of a single individual—Microsoft chairman Bill Gates—during this *one single day* would have been enough money to install basic computer labs in every public high school in America.

(Not to suggest anything here, just wondering: why don't poor people ever decide to gang up, march on up to Seattle, and just mug the guy? I'm not saying it would be a good idea. I'm not saying you should run out and do it right now. I'm not saying you should pick up the phone and start organizing everyone you know into a vigilante band of torch-wielding thugs and attack the Microsoft compound at dawn. Really, I'm not. I'm just asking.)

Incidentally, there's a silver lining to stock pullbacks they rarely mention on brokerage-sponsored CNBC programs, even though it's Econ 101:

Many folks who sweat for a living have much more money invested in their homes than in the stock market. And if things get really bad and truly big investors flee the market for safety, they buy (among other things) real estate, which drives property values up. Which is *good* for a large segment of the middle class. Inflation is the same deal. In the corporate media, it's considered 100 percent bad. But even if your paycheck doesn't quite keep up with inflation, so stuff like a gallon of milk gets a little harder to buy, you're also paying off a fixed-rate mortgage in cheaper and cheaper dollars. So you're not hurting as badly as the rich people on TV like to say you are, all considered.

Of course, if you're poor or renting, you're screwed. Just like always. And there are still plenty of negative things about stock pullbacks. I'm just saying that it's all a lot more complex than they say on TV. Particularly when they're panicking.

Then again, if most reporters can't handle basic arithmetic, you can't expect them to grok supply and demand.

For that you need expert commentators. And maybe a drum and some goat entrails.

It truly is a global economy.

At 9 a.m. Brazil devalues its currency, and by noon suddenly all our IRAs disappear faster than Hootie & the Blowfish.

Suprised? You shouldn't be. Look at the tags on the stuff you own. ILGWU labels are such a thing of the past that if you're under thirty, you probably don't even know what that stands for. (It's either "International Ladies' Garment Workers Union," or "I Love Gyrating in Women's Underwear." One or the other. I get confused.)

The only thing in your whole house that was made within 100 miles is probably your own children.

You hope anyway.

Meanwhile, travel to any of the countries you find listed on your collars and linings, and you'll find increasing chunks of corporate America. You can get McDonald's in Red Square, Kentucky Fried Chicken in Beijing, and really great New York bagels on the streets of Istanbul. Strangely, however, all the cab drivers in Turkey are from New Jersey. Must be some sort of exchange program.

The Maldives Islands—which I can barely even find on a map, and I was on *Jeopardy!*, people—recently banned the Disney movie *Prince Of Egypt* because it wasn't Islamic enough. The censorship made the newspapers, but I thought I saw a much bigger story: since when are they showing Disney movies in the Maldives Islands?

(Incidentally, they also banned *The Ten Commandments*, because it was too Jewish, and *Meet Joe Black*, because it sucked.)

Globalization is supposed to be a good thing in the long run, but I have my doubts. The same international trade agreements which

bring Taco Bell to Burundi also make it possible for twenty-three-year-old bond traders in London to move billions of dollars in and out of various countries in less time than it takes Jerry Seinfeld to pick up a prom queen.

And with half the planet in severe economic turmoil, where's a speculator supposed to get a reliable return on his money these days?

After years of easy money, Wall Street's looking about as fairly-priced as a tub of movie popcorn, and even more likely to cause a heart attack.

Not many other countries look safe for a killing, either. The Euro is declining, Latin America is always boom and bust, and most Asian markets are about as good an idea as the new *Kung Fu* TV series.

It's almost enough to make a professional investor go out and get a job.

But worry not, dear predators. I've been poking around, and there's still one place where your surplus money can reproduce like ebola:

Mongolia.

Remember 1997's Bloody Monday, when the Dow dropped 550 points, and almost every other market on the planet crashed at the same time? Mongolia was up six percent just that one day alone. In fact, the index of the top seventy-five stocks traded in Ulan Bator recently hit a mark of 332—up from about eighty-four less than two years ago. That's roughly a 100 percent annual return for the last two years.

And you thought Fidelity Magellan was hot stuff.

Turns out Mongolia is an Emerging Market player's paradise: post-communist monopolies with government subsidy, cheap labor, and no human rights inspectors. Somebody get Phil Knight on the phone—when he's done with Vietnam, Nike's got a new home up north.

For the truly greedy, Mongolia may be the best investment anywhere on Earth. Unless possibly there's a futures market in Antarctica. With global warming, maybe we can short the icecaps.

There's just one catch: the main reason the Mongolian Exchange was unaffected by other markets is that the country is just too darn isolated to move any money in or out of there. You want to invest in Mongolia? Fine. Grab a yak, exchange your dollars for a wheelbarrow of tugriks, and hit the trail.

Which explains why I saw Peter Lynch buying dry goods at Home Depot.

Still, I hope whoever's running the Mongolian stock market knows what they're doing. I don't know if my Keogh can afford a decline in the Tugrik. In which case, I'll have to spend my retirement years working for McDonald's.

Possibly in Botswana.

You might prefer to think it's just a leftist structural theory that labor and export market stability are often the underlying reasons for various U.S. sanctions, military actions, and other foreign policies. Or you can just read *Investor's Business Daily* and the like, where such things are often spelled out explicitly by the players themselves, with remarkably little concept that any other paradigm for human behavior might exist.

I've made exactly three calls on the direction of the stock market, ever. In the process of keeping abreast of the latest cruelties, I sometimes notice that a surprisingly large number of otherwise sophisticated people are acting like morons, more so than usual. And three times the thickness of the stupidity compelled me to comment.

All three were calling market tops, which are supposedly harder to forecast than a market rise, since historically the market usually goes up, although I think they're easier, since you can spot them whenever cabdrivers and stewardesses start waving their retirement cash around like extras making wagers in the Russian Roulette scene in *The Deer Hunter*.

The first call was published three months before a steep decline, the second was two days prior, and the last one was published literally the day before the drop.

I guess I have to make the next call just a few minutes early, which will mean giving all of you pagers.

Here they are in reverse chronological order:

January 1999

You tell me what's more valuable: the bookseller Amazon.com, which has yet to show a single dollar in profit and is dwarfed in many respects by several competitors, or…the country of Norway?

You guessed it.

As *Barron's* noted this week, do the math, folks, and according to the speculators now ruling the casino on Wall Street, the market capitalization of Amazon.com is now comparable to that of the *entire stock market of Norway*.

Does that sound reasonable to you?

It gets better.

Suppose for a second that Amazon.com had a complete monopoly on every book sold in the United States. The stock is still priced at *fifty times* the hypothetical earnings.

That's roughly five or ten times what the stock would sell for if it had a complete monopoly on every book in the United States.

Yahoo! is now trading at about $400. That's for a company posting earnings per share of about a penny a week.

If I knew a girl with a bubble this large, I'd ask her out.

Calling the exact timing of market movements is considered almost impossible, but two of the most powerful indicators of an impending downturn are:

a) the opinions of investment newsletters, and

b) the number of people buying call options, (a high-risk, high-reward way of betting the market's about to go up quickly) compared to those buying puts (a similar bet on an impending drop).

Both of these groups are notoriously wrong, so when you see all the newsletters going positive, or you see twice as many calls being bought than puts, that's usually a good time to start looking for the exits. If you see both at the same time, just hope you can get out before getting crushed in the melee.

Last week, volume in call options exploded.

The investment newsletters were more bullish than they've been in seven years.

Uh-oh.

If we were getting any closer to a crash, oxygen masks would be dropping onto the NYSE trading floor. Brokers would be bending over, putting their heads between their legs, and closing their eyes.

This is just one guy's opinion here, so take my advice at your own risk, but remember the last time I was this amused by stock overvaluations was just days before last summer's big pullback.

Do your own thinking, of course. Make your own decisions.

And then...RUN!!!!!!!

Partly thanks to blind luck, the day after the above was published, the Dow began a 500 point decline. Both Amazon and Yahoo! lost around forty percent of their value, although at press time they've rebounded slightly and are now down only about thirty percent.

A couple of days after the next wordpile was published, the Dow began its summer 1998 correction.

July 1998

Call my broker. I'm going long on tulips.

Y'know, there's no reason whatsoever to think that human beings are rational. I don't care if you're talking about Psychic Surgery, the Great Seattle Pitted Windshield Epidemic, or the fine musicianship of Celine Dion, we humans believe almost anything we feel like believing. Reality is just this sort of bumpy thing that gets in the way.

Backing up a second, Psychic Surgery is where a guy pretends to stick his hand in your belly and pull out cancers, when all he's really doing is palming a chicken giblet; the Seattle Pitted Windshield Epidemic was that time a few years ago when somebody noticed pits in his windshield that were always there, pointed it out, and everybody else noticed them too, so people freaked out because something weird was suddenly attacking their windshields; and as to Celine Dion—have you heard her cover of "All By Myself?" It's a song of complete emotional abandonment and despair, and she does it with a triumphant key change at the end, belting out these almost suicidal lyrics like she just discovered Cold Fusion. It's like a disco version of "Taps."

Ever heard of Tulip Mania? In 1630s Holland, speculators ran up the price of tulips to where eventually even a single bulb could buy you a decent sized house. Then around 1638 somebody noticed that, dude, it's a *tulip*. And the market crashed.

If you've heard the story before, it gets even better. What most people leave out is the sequel—Hyacinth Mania, which was when the Dutch went through the exact same thing 100 years later. I'm not making that up. Nobody learned a thing.

So…have you priced Internet stocks lately? Do the math.

Suppose your kid had an online business that made five cents a month. Would you pay him 200 bucks for it? With many Internet stocks, that's what people are doing. At best. Many Internet stocks have yet to earn a single dollar—in an industry where the only sure thing is that new technology changes everything every couple of years.

Heck, I'm starting my own Internet business, where you can see me do psychic surgery on pitted windshields while Celine Dion does a tap dance about suicide. The bidding begins now. See you online at www.tulipmania.com.

December 1996

The big news this week is on Wall Street, where stock traders have been enjoying more cheap highs than the road crew at a Cypress Hill show.

Most nights, the TV newsmodels proudly recite the Dow Jones Industrial Average like a winning sports score, accompanied by video footage of excited bald guys in Brooks Brothers suits messing up each other's combovers.

You're supposed to think happiness on Wall Street is good news for the rest of us.

Ain't necessarily.

Last week was a good example:

There's this thing called "momentum investing." Simply put, it's buying into whatever stock is going up really fast, assuming there must be a good reason, and trying to get back out before everybody else realizes there isn't.

Momentum players cause enormous temporary price gains, which in turn attracts more cash into the casino. People who think of themselves as too smart for the lottery pour their IRAs into mutual funds, and if there aren't any bargains, fund managers still have to put the money somewhere. So even some truly lousy stocks are still going up, and most folks are pretty happy.

That's why private companies like the Boston Celtics, Ticketmaster, and Super Wash (the car wash chain) are rushing to

go public: people are simply willing to pay more for their shares than they're probably worth.

(Somebody explain the growth potential here: Ticketmaster isn't any more likely to double the capacity of Comiskey Park than the Celtics are to begin franchising. And as for Super Wash, do you really want to sink your life savings into a company you can replace with a garden hose, a bucket, and a damp rag?)

The skyrockets make a pretty show, but by most historic pricing yardsticks—earnings, yield, book, etc.—the stock market is looking at about a fifteen percent drop just to reach a relatively normal value. That's about 1000 Dow points from here.

Yaaaaa.

That won't necessarily happen right away, if at all. Maybe prices will hold for a year as earnings catch up; maybe kablam tomorrow.

Maybe three more years of dancing on the ceiling, and then we party like it's 1999.

Anyhow, Federal Reserve Board Chairman Alan Greenspan, who speaks like an undertaker trained in hypnosis, recently made one single small mention of "irrational exuberance," hinting that stock prices just *might* be approaching speculative levels.

(Greenspan went on to theorize that cheese comes from cows, bowling balls roll, and *Millenium* is such turgid crap you wonder how come *The X-Files* is any good.)

Boom. Worldwide panic selling. 130 points off the Dow in thirty minutes.

Why all the fuss? Greenspan and the Fed can deworm the tequila at will, simply by raising interest rates a notch. That makes money itself more expensive, discouraging speculation.

Which would hurt business at the Harrah's on the Hudson.

Traders calmed down quickly, however. Some good news came in.

Read this next with bitter irony:

Fortunately for investors, "the Labor Department reported early Friday that non-farm payroll jobs grew by just 118,000 in November, and the nation's unemployment rate rose to a four-month high at 5.4 percent. The two figures suggested that the economy is slowing down, allaying some fears about rising interest rates."

Read that paragraph—which comes verbatim from CNN—again. Go on. You glazed the first time. Read it again.

To Wall Street, low job growth and surging unemployment are *good* news.

This is not unusual. It's just the most recent example.

Watch and read closely. Think for yourself. And prepare for shock:

Good news for Wall Street is surprisingly often bad news for you and me.

And vice versa.

Part V

Technology
Don't Sweat the Small Stuff, the Big Stuff's Gonna Kill You Anyway

Chapter Thirteen

The Cutting Edge Of Medicine
& Other Painful-Sounding Things

Losing weight isn't actually all that bloody difficult. You just eat less and exercise more. Of course, nobody ever got rich telling fat people *that*.

Bake a potato. You get 6 ounces of sodium-free, non-fat food bursting with Vitamin C, iron, copper, and wads of fiber. Cost: about thirteen cents.

Buy some Lay's potato chips. You still get six ounces—with little fiber, no minerals, gobs of sodium, and sixty percent fat calories. And it's only seven times as expensive as the genuine spud.

A no-brainer, right?

But wait! Now you can buy Frito-Lay's new Wow chips, made with Olestra, Procter and Gamble's new fat substitute! Wow chips are non-fat. Of course, so is the actual potato, and with Wow chips you're still paying seven times for road salt, a shiny bag, and an intestinal DuraLube.

And there's more. With Olestra, you can also get acute nausea, diarrhea, and anal leakage. Yum. And if you're really loyal, you risk dehydration, heart disease, cancer, and blindness. Mmm-mmm good.

Here's the deal: Olestra is a huge molecule, so large that the body hasn't the slightest clue what it is and wisely dumps it right out the back end. That's precisely why it's low-cal. And the way out, the molecule also binds to vital disease-fighting compounds called carotenoids. So Olestra actually removes existing nutrients from your body. It's negative food. Karen Carpenter's Dream Snack.

Frito-Lay (which sounds like something you do in the back of an El Camino) knows they're selling Ex-Lax Potato Leeches, but Wow chips, marketed as a healthy, low-fat product, are selling at the rate of over a million dollars' worth a day.

Never mind that hundreds of guano-munchers got a bad case of Frito Bandito's Revenge, and now consumer advocates are justifiably pissed off.

Of course, Procter & Gamble has tried to poo-poo the poo-poo, explaining—seriously—that "people experience gastrointestinal effects all the time."

Maybe when they eat *other* Procter & Gamble products, sure. Knock back a shooter of Biz, and, yeah, you'll cramp up. But P&G knew the dope, so their disclaimer is a lot like the Thalidomide folks saying, "people experience flipper effects every day."

That the FDA approved this crap—over objections from hundreds of doctors—only reveals the bankruptcy of the regulatory process. For decades now, many government watchdog agencies have been run by industry executives who decimate health and safety standards for their rapacious cohorts before returning to hefty waiting bonuses. The FDA, larded with food and chemical executives who stand to make a killing—literally—is no exception.

Still, to be fair to these giant corporations—silly me—while Olestra was still being test-marketed, I drove to Grand Junction, Colorado (one of three small test cities, coincidentally hundreds of miles from competent product liability attorneys) and tried a bag of what were then called "Max" chips myself, finding them in the filling station when I stopped to buy some gas.

Boy, did I ever.

(Before continuing the rest of this piece, go find a road atlas. Enjoy my pain.)

As you'll see on the map, looking west from Grand Junction, the cities get about as rare as a good Demi Moore movie. It's ninety minutes to Green River, Utah, and from there it's another 120 miles to anything else.

I munched as I drove. Max chips tasted pretty much the way all potato chips taste: like little salted Crisco biscuits. I wiped my lips and pressed on.

However, judging from the effect the chips had on my body, I can only presume that the name Wow was chosen only because the name Urrrrrggghhh was already taken.

I made it—barely—to Green River. I stayed up all night in Green River. And I caught up on a lot of reading. In the Green River Super 8, you can't see the TV from the bathroom.

My suggestion for the product's new slogan:

Betcha Can't Excrete Just One.

Shortly after I took the Electric Stomach Acid Test, the FDA approved the glop, but only after demanding the addition of a bunch of vitamins which might replace some of the stuff being pulled out of you, and also insisting on a warning label linking Olestra to everything from anal leakage to the Kennedy assassination.

However, the Center for Science in the Public Interest (CSPI) insists that long-term use of Olestra causes a lot more discomfort than Procter & Gamble admits, and eventually may cause thousands of cancers nationwide.

At a 1998 news conference, Dr. Walter Willett, head of the Department of Nutrition at Harvard's School of Public Health, stated that several studies correlate increased carotenoids with decreased cancers, and that "even the amount of olestra in a small, one-ounce bag of potato chips will lower blood carotenoids by over fifty percent if consumed on a daily basis."

CSPI wants the FDA to withdraw approval of the glop, make people like Frito-Lay stop selling the chips as "Fat Free," or at least strenghten the warning labels to include more stuff about cancer, blindness, and maybe Watergate or Iran-Contra.

For their part, Procter & Gamble admits that Olestra passes through you undigested and bonds to fat-soluble vitamins, but claims it's nothing to worry about. In their words, "there are still scientists that disagree...there is no study that has shown conclusively that carotenoids have any effect on health."

The tobacco guys said roughly the same thing for decades: as long as there are scientists who disagree (some of whom happen to be on our payroll), then there's no reason to listen to the head nutrition guy at Harvard.

At current consumption rates, the Harvard guy estimates that the U.S. will experience between 2,000 and 9,800 excess cases of prostate cancer, 32,000 excess cases of heart disease, 1,400 to 7,400 excess cases of lung cancer, and 80 to 390 excess cases of blindness.

In addition to some almost-normal-tasting chips.

The FDA has reportedly received over *five thousand* letters from people whose Olestra experiences were generally similar to mine: eating a bunch of chips and then having to Squeeze the Charmin for their very lives.

And the FDA reviewed Olestra again. And decided it was perfectly OK.

The FDA says they haven't *seen* anything that would cause them to change their minds.

Oh really? Apparently what they're asking for here is a visual aid.

Next time you suffer adverse side effects from consuming Olestra, maybe the best thing to do is simply place those adverse side effects in a sealed container, and send them directly to the FDA.

After all, fair's fair. It's nothing the government doesn't give us all the time anyway.

Here's a diet trade-off: actual sugar—but with half the calories and twice the flatulence.

Here we go again.

It'll be a few years before it's shrink-wrapped at the Kroger's, but a bunch of goggleheads at something called the Center for Plant Breeding and Reproduction Research—where I can only imagine a bunch of teutonic guys in armbands and boots converting Venus Fly Traps into military superweapons—have managed to dump a gene from the Jerusalem artichoke into the guts of a sugar beet, creating a new form of glucose you can:

a) eat, but

b) not fully digest.

Swell. Pop open a bag of Wow chips and just declare a goddamn festival, why not.

The Center says that the new sugar will also help prevent heart attacks and deaths from E Coli.

Well, sure. That's because the new stuff leaves your innards more confused than George Will at a Wu Tang concert, so while it's in your gullet a bunch of friendly bacteria drive up and dance around seductively and make more bacteria and eventually form big organic acids that kill bad bacteria and lower your cholesterol.

Right about here I'm realizing bacteria have a better social life than I do.

Trouble is, organic acids also create hydrogen gas. Which needs an escape route. And there's only two ways to go.

Either you explode like the Hindenberg...or you just sound like you might.

So the new sugar might help you get skinny enough to attract a really sexy mate. But they probably won't stay very long.

Bottom line: no matter how sweet the new stuff tastes, what movie producers call the Back End on the deal suffers from a bigger catch than Isadora Duncan.

Attention former Phen-Fen users: they can fix that scary side effect now—by punching a hole right through your heart.

You've probably already heard that the main concern about Phen-Fen was that it could lead to a really deadly heart thing called Primary Pulmonary Hypertension (PPH) which is this deal where really high pressure builds up in your lungs, your heart fails, and you drop dead.

Which, I suppose, *is* one way to lose a lot of weight, but it does seem kind of drastic.

Well, if you're one of the Kate Winsletts out there who gulped down a bunch of the stuff hoping to transform yourself into Kate Moss—and now you're afraid you'll wind up Peat Moss instead—there's good news. There's now a treatment for PPH.

A Mexico City doctor named Julio Sandoval (which anagrams into Loud Jon Saliva, a name I vastly prefer) is treating PPH using a procedure called "Graded Balloon Dilation Atrial Septostomy," which is docspeak for punching a small hole in the wall between the left and right sides of your heart, sliding a little balloon through the hole, and then inflating the balloon until the hole is just big enough to relieve the pressure.

Of course, you coulda just ate your dang veggies.

Surprisingly, Dr. Saliva's procedure actually works pretty well. It's no cure, but if you suffer through PPH without the deal, 50-50 you're dead in two years. But let the dude run a balloon through your ticker, and your odds go up to ninety percent.

Granted, it sounds unpleasant.

But then again, a lot of former Phen-Fen users are already walking around with balloons in their chests. What's one more?

Beauty may only be in the eye of the beholder, but that doesn't mean people won't just about kill themselves trying to catch that eye in the first place.

I live in West Hollywood, where some folks have had so many facelifts they share the same general expression as a largemouth bass. The Diet Foods section at the corner grocery always has one or two of these unblinking Lizard Women with noses that appear to have come from an entirely different edition than the rest of their head. It's like Microsoft just released their copy of Face 2.0 and they didn't get all of the update disks.

We guys have it pretty easy when it comes to appearances. All *we* have to be is anatomically correct, willing to listen, and not insane, and most women are willing to talk to us. Appearance counts, but basically, if you're free of parasites and not naked, you've got a shot at it.

Women, on the other hand, face ludicrous standards of beauty. It's not enough for *Playboy* and *Penthouse* to spend gazillions scouring the planet for genetic mutations they can repackage in spandex; then they gotta retouch the pictures, transforming the unlikely into the completely impossible.

Centerfolds in men's magazines ought to come with warnings, like cigarette packages: The Surgeon General Has Determined That These Women Do Not Exist.

But never mind. We still strive. There's underwear to make small parts look bigger and big parts look smaller. There's implants and nose jobs and even rib-removal surgery.

Trouble is, you can really hurt yourself looking good. Excessive exercise often causes severe injury. Surgeries go wrong. Phen-Fen can kill.

And now we discover that high-heeled shoes can ruin your knees. According to research out of Harvard Medical School, even 2.5-inch pumps, worn regularly, double the risk of arthritis of the knee.

I know a girl who says she always wears spike heels because a tottering, mincing walk brings out a guy's protective instincts. Um, girlfriend? Maybe so, but think how vulnerable you'll look in twenty years when you can't even walk down the street.

Maybe she can find a pair of black stiletto crutches. Gee, I feel protective already.

Or maybe, when we evaluate beauty, we can all try to honor the same oath that a lot of L.A. plastic surgeons seem to have long forgotten:

First, *do no harm.*

Stay up late one night, and you'll still see a dozen TV ads promising miracle products that block your body's ability to absorb fat, magically transforming your figure from Wilson Phillips to Peta Wilson to a Phillps screwdriver, and all in even less time than it takes Michael Flatley to look like a preening twit.

If you want to lose weight, you're better off changing channels and ordering the Nothing Down Real Estate Through Hypnotic Self-Improvement tapes. You'll soon be so poor you won't be able to afford food.

That said, scientists up at UC San Francisco have discovered a key enzyme that your body uses to produce fat molecules, and they think that coming up with a way to block that enzyme may not be far behind.

The enzyme is called DGAT, which stands for a chemical name that contains every letter of the alphabet, two bird calls, and a wide range of high-pitched clicking sounds. For weight-loss purposes, let's assume DGAT stands for Don't Glom Another Taco, and we'll be just fine.

DGAT normally combines with other molecules to form compounds called triglycerides, which make up about ninety-five percent of your excess flesh and one hundred percent of Charles Barkley's head.

So blocking DGAT would make it impossible for your body to manufacture fat.

What *would* come out of you instead isn't exactly clear yet, although I strongly suspect it'll show up in the next John Waters movie, possibly wearing eye shadow.

Anyway, actual skinny pills may only be five years away.

Which means side effects, mutations, and premature deaths are only ten years out. Lawsuits are fifteen years away, and self-help books for relatives in recovery should pop out around 2020.

Some people, however, are naturally thin. The bastards.

We all know people who can eat whatever they want and never seem to gain a pound. Occasionally we even let them live. I had a tall skinny friend in college who would eat his entire body weight in microwave burritos twice a day, and he had Abs of Steel. Me, I could start the day every morning with a quick jog around Ohio, and I'd still be entering the room belt buckle first.

But when I'm not jogging, I tend to sit relatively still. My skinny friend was always in motion—pulling at his hair, adjusting his glasses, vibrating quietly, or occasionally hovering in midair and gathering nectar with his flute-like beak.

Turns out all the extra activity was probably why he was so skinny. That and the power sander he used to buff with in the shower.

New research by a team at the Mayo clinic indicates that all that squirming and twitching some people do burns calories and keeps them thin.

They call the excess fiddling around "non-exercise activity thermogenesis," or NEAT, because acronyms help make sure researchers get paid.

Anyhow, fidgety people tend to look like candles before they're lit, while calm people tend to look more like the wax left behind.

So, bottom line—if you're nervous about losing weight…that's half the battle.

And then there are people who are thin because there's something wrong with their brain. And I don't mean anyone I ever dated, although the thought did cross my mind.

Anorexia and bulimia are easy for male comedians to joke about, because we don't get it. In both senses of that phrase. And they're often accompanied by depression, so it just looks to an outsider like some spoiled, pouty rich girl is too vain to be bothered to eat.

But a growing body of research says that a lot of this stuff is linked to a deficiency of serotonin, the brain's natural happy drug. High serotonin, you feel like the shower scene from *Singin' In The Rain*. Low serotonin, you feel more like the shower scene from *Psycho*.

I was once briefly very close to an anorexic young lady—a comedian, of all things—who I'm convinced had a little less serotonin than Sylvia Plath. Thanks to her difficulty managing her own moods, she was simultaneously one of the sweetest and most difficult people I've ever known. Eventually we stopped being friends, which still makes me sad. Stuff like this really affects people's lives bigtime.

But a new study from Oxford says dietary intake of the amino acid L-tryptophan alleviates a lot of the symptoms. The FDA yanked supplemental tryptophan off the market after there was a single bad batch a few years ago, but you can still get it by taking 5-hydroxytryptophan supplements, or simply eating most veggie protein sources like pumpkin seeds, nuts, and tofu. I've put a list of happy foods on my website, www.bobharris.com.

(Note to keep my lawyer happy: this is not medical advice. See your doctor before making any changes in your dietary habits, clothing, or hairstyles. Keep away from fire or flame. May cause drowsiness. Do not use as a floatation device.)

I never did reach my friend with the hope things could truly change profoundly and for the better. But if someone you love suffers from an eating disorder or related depression, there's hope.

They may not be out of their gourd. They may just need to eat some of the seeds.

There are other causes of depression, too. For example, you might just be missing part of your brain.

According to a new study from Washington University in St. Louis, some depressed folks are simply missing a few strategic brain cells.

That doesn't mean the converse, that everyone with missing grey matter is necessarily depressed. Otherwise there wouldn't be so much cheering at tractor pulls.

But doctors have known for a while that some cases of inherited depression may be caused by getting shortchanged in your subgenual prefrontal cortex (SPC), a dime-sized piece of brain behind the center of your forehead, right where your Third Eye would be if you were a John Tesh-listening, crystal-handling, New Age moron.

And the new study indicates that in many people with manic-depression, there's a shortage of glia, which are cells that schlep around and get coffee for your thinking neuron cells, and whose response to serotonin is a major factor in whether you feel like hugging that Jehovah's Witness or scoring his aorta with a steak knife.

So there's a definite genetic component to some forms of depression, and it's one that many current drug therapies simply aren't yet designed to cope with.

Not that this is all such a surprise. I mean, look:

Aaron Spelling.

Tori Spelling.

See? Obviously, the cause of depression can be reproduced. Except in that case we're the ones getting depressed.

———————————

Are you ever worried because you can't remember things?

Your worry is probably part of why you can't remember things.

Researchers at the University of California at Irvine have recently proven that there's a direct link between stress and the inability to remember stuff.

Which I've been reminded of a lot lately.

As you're surely sick of hearing, I once got all the way to the final of the *Jeopardy!* Tourney o' Champs, and then got creamed by a professor from Berkeley.

Believe it or not, I still get recognized amazingly often. Some days I can't buy a box of cereal without somebody in line saying, "Hey, you're that *Jeopardy!* guy…boy, did you get creamed."

Yeah, thanks. Thanks for reminding me.

The new study makes sense to me now, however. Stress was one of the main reasons I lost.

Stress, and a bunch of categories like:

> Things Bob Doesn't Know
>
> Things Bob Used To Know, But Forgot
>
> Things Bob Never Heard Of
>
> Things Only One Person On Earth Knows, And He Lives In Cambodia, and
>
> Restaurants In Berkeley.

I'm not even bothering with the buzzer at this point; I'm searching the podium for an Eject button.

Anyway.

Stress.

It makes you forget things.

Stress makes your body secrete a bunch of hormones called glucocorticoids, which are great for speeding your reflexes—just in case you need to fight off a sharp-toothed predator, for example—but don't do squat for your memory.

In fact, glucocorticoids pretty much block the whole memory process entirely. Which makes sense from an evolutionary standpoint: you don't really need to remember John Quincy Adams while you're wrestling with a puma.

Which means that the more you struggle to remember something—which causes stress—the less chance you have of actually remembering anything.

Take it from one who knows.

Not getting enough sleep crosses our wires as well.

This is an actual headline from a genuine Reuters news story:

"Sleep Deprivation Affects Surgical Skill."

Dateline: Planet Obvious.

Indeed, acording to British investigators at the Imperial College School of Medicine at St. Mary's in London, "Lack of sleep may affect performance in the operating theatre."

I assume they mean for the surgeon. Although if you're a patient, not getting to sleep would seem like just as big a problem.

The research was done by messing with a bunch of doctors' sleep schedules and then having them do a virtual reality simulation of a surgical procedure called "laproscopic cholecystectomy."

I'm not sure what that is either, but if I remember my Latin prefixes, it has something to do with grafting a rabbit onto your keister.

And *Ta-Da!* Surgeons who had no sleep the night before made twenty percent more errors than the rested ones. Not to mention all the deep grooves they cut in the operating table itself.

So why waste time documenting the self-evident? There's actually a sane reason for doing research into whether complete exhaustion might be a bad idea when playing mumblety-peg with somebody's innards.

Thanks to the demands of managed care programs in the UK and US, surgeons are being required to work longer and longer shifts. Which patients don't like much, seeing how they usually like to survive and all. Picky, picky.

However, before some bureaucrat can decide that maybe *Night Of The Living Dead* doesn't belong in the operating theatre, he needs something on paper to show his idiot boss and shareholders.

So there you are. Conclusive proof that doctors are, indeed, human.

Great. Now if only I can get someone to remove this rabbit.

Then again, neurochemistry affects us to the happy side, too. Like if you get so excited watching TV sports that you scream and high-five and generally act like a guy in a beer commercial, there's a good reason for your behavior:

You're on drugs.

At least that's what new research from the University of Utah indicates. And folks in Utah know a lot about altered brain chemistry. These people once thought Donny & Marie were an actual musical group.

See, labcoats have known for years that male athletes get a major testosterone boost from winning a competition, while the guys on the losing team actually suffer a drop in testosterone levels.

Y'know that whole deal where guys in a big event freak out a little and take things too seriously, like their manhood itself is on the line? On a neurochemical level, it *is*.

And it turns out that the same thing is true for couch potatoes at home just watching the game on the drool box. You root for Michael Jordan, your testosterone levels get a twenty percent boost. Root for the Denver Nuggets, and you go home feeling like four-fifths of a man.

Ever wonder why winning fans often go downtown and riot, while the losers (who you'd think would be acting out their frustrations) sit quietly at home and whimper into their herbal tea?

It's the testosterone. The winners are drunk out of their minds on it. The losers are running about a quart low.

Maybe next year the Florida Marlins should carry Viagra at the concession stands.

THIS MODERN WORLD

by TOM TOMORROW

Speaking of weird science, it had to happen: Viagra has won its creators the Nobel Prize.

Usually, when they give out the Nobel Prizes in the sciences, you and I have absolutely no shot at knowing what exactly the big deal is. For example, last year's prize in Physics went to the guys who expanded human understanding of something called the Fractional Quantum Hall effect, which is no relation to Anthony Michael Hall, even though the latter did star in the movie *Weird Science*, which is in the first sentence of this piece.

(I like M.C. Escher a lot. Can you tell?)

Make no mistake: Anthony Michael Hall is not a subatomic phenomenon. His film career only makes it seem that way.

Anyhow, what the physics dudes discovered is a totally new state of matter: when electrons under powerful magnetic strain interact with each other, the result is a set of particles that are mere fractions of what we started with.

This reminds me of nothing so much as a support group for divorced men.

This year's Nobel Prize in Medicine is another matter entirely. The million dollars goes to the three Americans who discovered the role of nitric oxide as a signaling device in your bloodstream. Which has applications in treating heart disease and infections and cancer and stuff. And that's really cool.

And that's not why they won the Nobel Prize.

Let's get real. The nitric oxide thing also led to the invention of Viagra.

And who hands the prizes out?

A bunch of rich old men.

A bunch of rich old men in Stockholm.

A bunch of rich old men in Stockholm who go every day of their lives surrounded by beautiful young Swedish women.

And somebody invents Viagra? *Of course* they win the Nobel Prize. I'm surprised they weren't named King. This'll be the first awards ceremony where they don't just hand out the medals, they carry the winners on their shoulders down the street.

Too bad nobody out there has invented a pheromone extract that makes young Swedish women feel attracted to these guys.

I guess now we know how to win next year's Chemistry prize.

Thinking of attraction as "chemistry" is hardly an exaggeration.

You've probably had this experience: you meet someone and instantly feel an amazingly intense attraction that you can't explain rationally. If you're lucky, it's mutual, and the two of you soon explore the frontiers of yoga while finding uses for a Lay-Z-Boy that Bob Vila never imagined. If you're unlucky—one of you is spoken for, or maybe you work in the Oval Office—you either have to struggle to forget it or risk being scorned by millions via satellite by Geraldo.

Writers have called this attraction "chemistry" ever since King John codified standard English clichés in the 1624 Banalbook of

Midbrow-On-Hackney. And apparently, King John's term is accurate. Some University of Chicago guys have finally proved the existence and power of human pheromones, the odorless chemicals which influence our mating habits.

Now let's not get carried away here. Smell isn't the only factor in attraction, although if you've spent much time on public transportation, you know it can be the cause of repulsion. There are other factors at work, too, most of which are primarily visual. When I was fourteen, I didn't put that Farrah Fawcett poster up because I liked the way the paper smelled.

But assuming that your potential partner is anatomically correct and generally free of obvious personality defects—which in L. A. can be a tall order—the subtle smells of love *can* be the deciding factor determining whether the two of you kiss each other good night or good morning.

In fact, some research indicates nature knows what it's doing: the exact composition of your pheromones may be a subtle message containing information about your health, genetic make-up, and immune system, and so the mutual yee-hah of love may just be nature's way of encouraging us to select partners whose contrasting make-up gives us the best chance to create healthy offspring.

So if you're talking with someone you're interested in, and suddenly it feels like there's something in the air—there probably is. In fact, deep breathing at that point might just lead to, uh, more deep breathing.

However, while you're doing that heavy breathing, here's an important tip:

Do Not Inhale Exploding Bugs.

You know those electrical bug zapper thingies that people hang in the backyard, punctuating midwestern summer barbecues with the constant *bzzt* of mosquitoes getting the Chair?

Supposedly these zappers are saving us from various insect-borne diseases, but sometimes the things are so gross I'd rather just go ahead and have the malaria.

When I was a kid, the state of the art was the No Pest Strip, which was really just poisoned sticky tape in a cardboard box, essentially a Roach Motel you could dangle like insecticidal mistletoe. They were everywhere in the Nixon years. Sometimes you'd even see these things hanging in restaurants, which was like a giant yellow sign flashing Just Order A Soft Drink And Move On.

But at least the Strips didn't call attention to themselves. They simply waited quietly for their prey, and if you weren't looking, you never knew when they moved in for the kill.

The big blue electrical thingies, on the other hand, are proud hunters, announcing each new conquest with a proud ZOT that tells you how large a catch they just made. *Dzzzt* means it's just a gnat. *Spzz-sztz*, and you've probably got yourself a moth. *BRAAAZZZOWNT!*, and that's either a Monarch Butterfly or possibly a small dog.

And now it turns out that dog may well have died in vain.

A professor of biology at Kansas State University (where apparently there isn't much to do besides look at bug zappers) has discovered that:

a) when the zapping occurs, the insects literally explode;

b) bacteria from the insect can be hurled as much as six feet, thereby posing a health risk to anyone nearby; and finally

c) only about one percent of the electrocuted bugs are even guilty of biting anybody. The other ninety-nine just show up at the wrong time and get fried.

Not that c) matters much in Florida or Texas.

How much of a problem is it? Since so few of the exploded bugs ever would have gone near a human being, the professor is convinced that bug zappers actually cause more disease than they prevent.

So, bottom line: if you find yourself near a large bug about to burst into flames, *do not inhale.*

President Clinton should do the Public Service Announcements.

Chapter Fourteen

Beware the Ides of the March of Science

I'm constantly amazed at how rapidly technology advances.

Fifteen years ago when I was in college (a depressing introductory clause if there ever was one), I went to one of the better engineering schools in the country. And we didn't have cell phones and fax machines and laptop computers. We didn't even have portable phones or consumer copiers or even the 3-inch floppy disk.

We lived like animals.

The state of the art in home computing was the Commodore 64, which had enough memory that it could handle *a graphic*. Singular.

The Commodore had only slightly more processing power than the box it came in.

I spent months and years of my life studying computer languages like Fortran and Algol and APL. I would have been better off learning Aramaic. I'd be more likely to use it in my current gig, and I would have met the cute girls from the liberal arts school.

My senior project was designed around state-of-the-art million dollar technology that you get now as a bonus when you subscribe to *Sports Illustrated*.

My degree means *nothing*. I have an honors level of knowledge about technology from 1984. Programming in Java? I'm a complete novice. But when that Pong game breaks down, I'm the man to call.

My VCR actually tells the correct time.

That only cost me $40,000.

That's why I became a writer. A writer's work doesn't suddenly become completely obsolete. (Unless you work for the WB, where most producers require your work to start out that way.) For most

writers, it's not like you turn thirty and some kid right out of college looks at you and says, "You're still using verbs?"

I'm a low-tech guy now, largely because I *know* that nothing high-tech I learn or buy is going to be worth anything in five to ten years.

So last year, the Galaxy 4 satellite suffers brainfreeze and rotates a few degrees off axis. Of course, I do the same thing when I see Toni Braxton. But the Galaxy 4 lock-up was a little more important than mine. One computer glitch, and suddenly 40 million people can't function without pagers which they didn't even have five years ago.

If we don't learn our lesson, next time can only be worse.

How much you wanna bet that one computer error someday crashes the whole human race, because no one will be able to live without a device that you and I have never heard of yet?

Forget *Deep Impact*. The real end of the world will be titled *Cancel, Abort, Retry*.

I like to think of myself as an environmentally-friendly guy, but I'm really a massive hypocrite.

Between my computer and my Internet hookup and the radio on all day and the cable TV and the little vibrating thing I like to wear on my, uh, shoulders, I probably use almost as much electricity as the Florida justice system.

So I worry about where the energy comes from. Nuclear power? Too bad about those 100,000 years of toxic leftovers. Oil? Maybe, if they'd stop forging tanker hulls out of the captains' leftover beer cans. And don't even talk to me about coal. One of my grandfathers was a coal miner. He had lungs like a Brillo pad. When his hair went grey, he didn't buy Grecian Formula, he just coughed on his comb.

Which is why I continue to advocate the development of more sustainable sources of power: wind turbines, biomass and geothermal generators, hydroelectric plants, and a national initiative to recapture the petroleum content of Cher.

Dream with me, people.

Most of all, I'm rooting for solar power. Properly developed, solar power will be clean, cheap, and inexhaustible. In other words, pretty much what Clinton expected from his intern program.

Unfortunately, for years you only saw solar power used in really desolate, hopeless locations almost no one visits, like a remote pay phone, a billboard in the desert, or Magic Johnson's late night talk show.

But through little fault of the major energy companies, solar power is finally becoming viable as a large-scale source of power. And as a demonstration to the people of Los Angeles, the Ferris Wheel down at the Santa Monica pier is getting hooked up.

Finally, the future we read about as kids is about to arrive.

Solar Ferris Wheels! Solar public buses and trains! And in Florida, the sunshine state, the ultimate liberal conundrum:

Solar electric chairs!

Talk about good news and bad news...

I watched *Star Trek* a lot when I was a kid. It was the Future, with transporter beams and phaser guns and space women in plastic miniskirts. I couldn't wait to grow up. But now when I see reruns, it's striking how many of the high-tech devices actually now exist. The two-way videoconferencing is no big deal anymore. Those really cool flip-open communicators are really nothing more than cell phones with unlimited calling areas. And as far as plastic miniskirts go, modern skirt technology now exceeds William Shatner's most wild-eyed dreams.

On *Star Trek* they also had these way cool computers that talked in a sexy voice. Actually, if you listened closely, it was the same lady who played Nurse Chapel. Which made me worry sometimes that maybe I'd missed an episode and Nurse Chapel had been sucked into the computer and couldn't get out. Sort of like what happens to my nephew when he logs onto the Internet.

Anyway. The ChapelMatic 3000, or whatever it was called, was able to identify people by analyzing their fingerprints, voiceprints, and optic nerve patterns.

Experts have a special word for identifying people by their physical characteristics: *biometrics*. Experts need a special word for something like this because experts like to get paid, and special words are one way to look like you know something worth paying for.

Anyhow, all of a sudden, Compaq and a bunch of smaller companies are marketing fingerprint readers for computer workstations, cheaply enough that it won't be long before a lot of companies start buying these things to enhance security around the office.

Which means that next time you go in to work in the morning, there's a good chance you won't even be able to get started without extending one of your fingers.

I used to have that problem, too.

Which is why I never worked anywhere very long.

Scientists in Copenhagen have created literally the smallest microprocessor possible: a computer chip where a single atom jumps back and forth to generate binary code, much the same way Anne Heche generates publicity.

The four-man team of goggleheads who accomplished this used a scanning-tunneling microscope to remove one of a single pair of hydrogen atoms from the surface of a silicon chip, leaving the remaining hydrogen atom available for further use.

Not surprisingly, not one of them have ever touched a girl.

What this means is that in ten years, storage density will increase by a factor of over a *million*. Within our lifetimes, it's actually possible that the entire sum of literature, art, music, and literally all human expression might eventually be stored on a single disc.

Which Bill Gates will own.

But then again, a lot of scientific advances are actually good things. For example, I fly about once a week, and I never give it a second thought anymore.

My travel agent knows to get me an aisle seat and a veggie meal, which is great. Although somehow she always books me in the Psychotic Toddler section, where ordinary two-year-olds channel Vlad the Impaler.

Halfway through the flight the stewardess always asks if I want a pillow.

So far I've said no.

Anyhow, the major airlines carried six hundred fifteen million people in 1998, and not *one* of us came to a premature end, pillows or no.

Some of it's just luck, and some of it is due to technological improvements in equipment in the air and on the ground. All of which is cool.

Politicians, however, like to credit the increased safety to the new anti-terrorist measures, wherein they:

a) ask if you packed your bags yourself, just in case you let a member of the Islamic Jihad roll your underwear;

b) ask if you kept your bags with you, just in case you loaned your stuff out to some guy wearing a Kaiser helmet you met in the washroom;

c) examine your laptop like a nearsighted urologist.

Every time I take my portable computer through airport security these days, not only do I have to prove it works (which is always dicey since the darn thing is so old, my version of Windows is stained glass—thank you! tip your waitstaff), I also have to stand there while they rub a cotton swab all over the thing, which is supposed to detect high explosives or drugs or Bill Clinton's DNA.

But I don't mind, since I'm not all that keen to get blown up in response to some other bombing half a planet away I had very little to do with. Particularly since I usually fly Southwest, where in the event of a forced landing you have to blow up the escape slides yourself.

You gotta love Southwest. Finally, someone has combined all the dangers of air travel with the creature comforts of a Greyhound bus. Southwest is like riding the back of somebody's pick-up truck at 30,000 feet. All I need is a bale of hay to lean on, a chicken in my lap, and a big hunting dog licking my neck, and my business trip on Southwest is complete.

I digress.

But the good news is some physicist guys in the UK have invented a new device called the Prismscope, which uses lasers to determine the chemical composition of any substance all the way down to the molecule. So the skies are about to get safer. The inventors say it can detect an explosive the size of a pinhead in a football stadium.

Which sounds a lot like Bill Romanowski.

So anyhow, the skies are safe. Although let's not get cocky. It's already crowded up there, and air traffic is gonna double in the next couple decades.

Which means the next big concern might not be mechanical failure, it might be something more like road rage. The only people sneaking guns through the metal detectors might be...the pilots.

As you surely know, scientists have cloned the first adult mammal. Human cloning will surely follow.

We're facing some big new questions.

Since cloning will be expensive at first, won't only rich people be cloned? Will Donald Trump breed in the wombs of 289 Puertoriquenas from Bayonne who need the money? Is it possible that 100 years from now entire cities will be named Perot and Forbes?

If not, won't clones still be considered status symbols, displayed at cocktail parties and on the cover of *InStyle* magazine? Or will the replication of the rich simply dilute their wealth?

Will a black market arise, where the poor can get a back-alley clone?

Will actually *being* a clone therefore carry a certain élan? Or will it be more declassé, like owning a print of an oil painting instead of the original?

Once cloning can begin *in utero*, how will we tell clones from originals? Dental records? Tattoos? Certificates of Authenticity we carry with our Driver's Licenses?

Will clones be subconsciously considered disposable? Will killing a clone carry less of a stigma than murdering the original?

How long until some rich guy creates lobotomized "spares" to replace his own aging human body parts? Will cruel parents hire surrogates and have their children in batches of four and five, so there are extras if one gets hit by a car?

What Social Security numbers do clones get? Do we just add a letter to the donor's number, starting with A for the first clone, B for the second, and so on?

Since most replicants will be born into undeserved wealth, will we see outbreaks of envious blue-collar clone-bashing? Will clones, like other oppressed groups, develop a system of non-verbal behaviors— e.g., wearing lapel pins shaped like rubber stamps—to signify their status? Will clones develop a national support group (ACNE: Adult Children of Nobody, Exactly) and a distinct vernacular ("eclonics")?

In school, why shouldn't clones be allowed to copy on exams?

Since only a small percentage of clone-fertilized eggs survive the process, how long until pro-lifers begin bombing chemistry labs?

Since DNA can be slyly collected from things like used Kleenex, how long until someone is cloned against their will? Will it be a crime? With what punishment? Who gets custody of the clone?

Will professional sports have strict anti-cloning rules? If not, how much will Michael Jordan's toenail clippings be worth?

Will cloning a second set of kids become a custody option in divorce proceedings? If someone who has been cloned dies without a will, who gets the stuff? The family, or the clone?

If a clone has *deja vu*, how can he tell?

If one accepts the Catholic notion of new-soul-at-conception, when exactly does a clone's soul form? If without conception there's no new soul, does the clone timeshare one with the original? What happens if the donor is Saved and the replicant isn't? Does St. Peter flip a coin, or what?

If clones have no soul, can they sing Gospel music convincingly?

Since DNA can be recovered from the dead, what's the status of the clone's soul then?

Since clones can be born to a virgin mother, would they therefore be Holy? How long until someone attempts to validate the Shroud of Turin by scraping off some DNA, raising the kid, and seeing if he can transform water into wine? If a Jesus Clone goes to church, will he sit in the audience or onstage? When he starts advocating humility, pacifism, and aid to the needy, how long until he gets crucified?

Since DNA evidence will become all but meaningless, what will Barry Scheck do for a living?

If a woman has a *menage a trois* with her husband and his clone, has she violated her wedding vows? Is a child sired by the clone illegitimate?

Masturbation isn't generally considered a crime. How about touching your clone in a sexually arousing way?

And how long until cloning is outlawed by male-dominated legislatures—just as soon as they realize that women no longer need them?

This just in: some researchers at Cal Tech are screwing around with the genetic blueprint of the *Drosophilia melanogaster* fruit fly.

I know you can barely contain your excitement.

Stay with me here. Believe me, this hurts me more than it hurts you. You have no idea how much crap I have to read to find these little pieces every freakin' day. Sometimes I sneeze and newsprint comes out my nose.

Anyway, the fruit fly geeks have discovered that the little buggers' lifespans and ability to react to stress both seem to be linked to a specific gene, a mutation they call the "Methuselah" gene.

Methuselah fruit flies live about a third longer than your average fruit fly, although that's still not long enough to get an operator when you call an airline. And it turns out the Methuselah flies also survive stress a lot better, which is probably why they live longer.

The scientists discovered this by subjecting the poor fruit flies to starvation, heat, and various horrifying toxins, thus proving conclusively that scientists need to get out more.

Anyhow, it turns out there's a similar Methuselah gene in worms—I mean, some of these science people could really use some sun—and so a lot of aging experts now think that a similar gene might exist in humans as well.

Or at least that's the opinion of one of the directors of the National Institute on Aging, Dr. David Finkelstein.

Dr. Frankenstein—excuse me, Dr. *Finkelstein*—thinks that if they can find the human Methuselah gene, then they can play with it and tweak it and build on it and thereby create a better, stronger, überhuman.

I do not like where this is going.

Suppose they eventually find this Methuselah gene in humans. Suppose they figure out how to get it turned on. And suppose the procedure is available outside the laboratory.

Who's gonna benefit? Working people like you and me, or the same bunch of banker wankers and beltway bandits who benefit from everything else?

If you've seen the movie *Cocoon*, yes, sure, it's fun to imagine a good long soak in the longevity pool.

But who wants to live forever if you have to spend eternity next to Pat Buchanan wearing a Speedo?

Hey, are you OK? You look kind of pale.

Oh. The Speedo thing. Yeah. Sorry.

Here. Take a couple of minutes and go do something until that last visual gets out of your head.

Go on. Take a walk. You're not breathing right.

Really. I'll be here when you get back.

All better? Good.

Now just don't look back at that last piece. Just keep reading. Relax. You're gonna make it. And try not to watch *Crossfire* for a few days. You'll be OK.

Chapter Fifteen

Military Waste
Let's Just Give the Pentagon All the Bubble Wrap and Call it Square

Here's why a lot of people just plain don't trust the military:

You've surely heard about the tragedy in Aviano, Italy, where a U.S. jet cut the wire supporting a ski-lift gondola, causing twenty people to fall to their deaths.

You'd surely hope that afterward, somebody in the military would have stepped forward right away, explained what happened, and accepted responsibility in an honorable manner.

You'd hope.

Brigadier General Guy Vanderlinden (who I loved on *Barney Miller*) is the deputy commander of NATO naval strike support forces in southern Europe. So this General Vanlederhosen guy is explaining after the accident how a state-of-the art EA-6B Prowler could happen to plow right into the cable supporting this ski lift and kill all these people. And this is what he said, direct quote:

"I do not believe the pilot diverted from the approved route."

Oh.

OK, General Vanlandingpad, let's see if I've got this straight: you're saying that his approved route was directly *into* this ski lift.

Y'all planned it that way.

As a training exercise, just in case Saddam Hussein equips the Republican Guard with ski lifts and gondolas. You've got a countermeasure.

I see.

The Italians didn't buy it. They said the pilot was miles off line and flying way too low. Which, after a bunch of denials, the Pentagon eventually admitted. And then they let the guy off anyway.

The Marines also denied that the plane had a flight data recorder. Which they turned over to the Italians a couple of days later.

Will the Pentagon ever learn? What happened in Aviano was an accident. What happened afterward wasn't.

And *that's* why a lot of people don't trust the military.

Also, a lot of the stuff that's supposed to protect us all doesn't and can't. And everybody knows it, and everybody still pretends otherwise.

I grew up in Ohio. It rains a lot. It snows. It sleets and hails and tornadoes. We get stuff some folks in California wouldn't even know the words for, like "virga" and "lake effect" and "black ice" and "whiteout." And you know what? Ain't no big thing. You wear a coat. You press on and make do.

In the real world, a cold wind and a little water in the sky is part of life pretty much everywhere human beings live on the entire planet.

The real world, of course, is a somewhat alien place to the Pentagon.

Y'know those B-2 Stealth Bomber planes you and I have been paying for all these years, the ones that cost a few billion bucks a pop, even before dealer prep and destination charges and the AM/FM cassette and all that?

Turns out they're even a more ridiculous rip-off than we thought. The General Accounting Office reports that to keep the stealth coating in place, the Stealth, quote, "must be sheltered or exposed only to the most benign environments—low humidity, no precipitation, moderate temperatures."

Funny, I have a diabetic uncle who needs the exact same conditions. He can barely make it to the bathroom, much less make a bombing run at Mach 2.

Let's get this straight: water—like the kind that falls from the sky everywhere in the world—makes the B-2 lose its magic vestments. Two H's and an O.

That's not exactly a countermeasure we can embargo.

The GAO also says the Air Force now believes that it's unlikely the problem, quote, "will ever be fully resolved." I was hoping maybe a can of ScotchGard and maybe a dab of Rain-X on the windshield would do the trick, but apparently not.

So the Air Force no longer plans to station any bombers overseas. Instead, they say the B-2 can still perform its mission by flying anywhere from their climate-controlled base in Missouri.

Unless, of course, they have to fly over Ohio. Or anywhere else where it might be raining.

So where is the outrage? This is a multi-*billion* dollar scandal—literally tens of thousands of times larger than any coffee deal in the White House.

Memo to the Pentagon: next time we have a war, make sure it's nice out.

"They call the RTGs indestructible…just like the Titanic was unsinkable…The Titan IV has blown up before. If it blows up this time and it releases plutonium, it will be too late to do anything about it whatsoever."

—Alan Kohn, thirty-year NASA veteran and
former chief of Emergency Preparedness

NASA is now in the habit of launching plutonium on top of a vehicle that blows up as predictably as Mike Tyson.

The Cassini probe is planned to take seven years en route to another four years of bobbing around Saturn's rings and moons. If all goes OK, we'll get some neato scientical factulation resolving all those burning questions you've been asking yourself about, um, Saturn's rings and moons.

Trouble is, the goshdurn thing's batteries are powered by plutonium-238, an isotope 280 times more radioactive than the stuff in nuclear warheads. As the plutonium decays, the ambient heat is converted into electric power by gizmos that NASA calls Radioisotope Thermoelectric Generators (RTGs). Nifty idea.

Plutonium-238—appropriately abbreviated Pu—is just about the most toxic substance in the universe. It's like someone crushed my most recent ex into a fine powder. Which is actually a pretty good idea.

Inhaled or ingested, plutonium irradiates nearby tissues, even as tiny amounts are meanwhile transported by the blood throughout the body. The results range from leukemia to bone, liver, and lung cancer. Plutonium particles can also cause thalidomide-like birth defects, genetic mutations, chromosomal defects, and other fine horrors.

Pu-238 is so hazardous that the U.S. doesn't even make it anymore; instead, we buy it from the Russians, who apparently didn't learn much from Chernobyl. Invisibly small amounts can kill; a sugar packet of the stuff could hypothetically wipe out Indianapolis. Which would be bad now that they have the new mall and everything.

The Cassini probe contains more than *seventy-two pounds* of plutonium.

Evenly distributed, that's hypothetically enough bad atoms to induce cancers in every person on Earth almost 100 times over.

And NASA strapped it all to a rocket that blows up sometimes.

Cassini was launched atop a Lockheed Martin Titan IV rocket. At the time of Cassini's launch, eighteen out of nineteen Titan IVs have lifted off OK.

The other one blew up real good.

Food for thought: Lockheed Martin also made the F-117 Stealth Fighter that inexplicably flew apart and crashed while flying level in perfect weather at an airshow in Maryland a few years ago, the aeronautic equivalent of spinning out of control and totalling your car while backing out of the driveway.

I mean, yeesh.

But not to worry, NASA said. Even if the Titan blows on liftoff, NASA pegged the chances of a plutonium release at 1 in 1400. Oh really? NASA also said the chance of a catastrophic event with a space shuttle was under one in 100,000—at least until the Challenger went blooey.

Credibility? Hello?

To keep Cassini's Pu from dispersing in a launch explosion or a re-entry fireball, its plutonium is cast into a ceramic form that makes it insoluble in water and less likely to disintegrate into a inhalable dust; the ceramic is then encased in heat-resistant layers of iridium and graphite. As a result, NASA says that RTGs are dispersal-proof up to about 4500 degrees Celcius.

Impressive? Eh, not really, no. Besides reaching local temperatures approaching that melting point, real explosions also create high-speed shrapnel and huge waves of overpressure. Even if the containers don't melt, the heat-softened and pressure-weakened casings might be easily blasted by high-velocity shrapnel which in tests can reportedly pierce the containers *even at room temperature*.

In short, plutonium release might be terribly more likely than NASA admits.

NASA also claimed any radiation would be contained to a small area near the launch pad. Not necessarily. In nuclear power plant accidents—which also occur at ground level, remember—radiation has travelled thousands of miles from the original accident. Fallout from Chernobyl was tracked over Europe and the U.S., both of which experienced a surge in thyroid cancers. England's 1957 Windscale disaster sent a radioactive cloud as far south as Cairo.

The good news: the Cassini probe was launched successfully. The respected rocket scientists expressing concern for public safety were written off as alarmists, and the media moved on.

Whew.

The bad news: the *very next* Titan IV rocket launch went kablooey, turning into a giant fireball forty seconds after launch and showering over a billion dollars' worth of fiery crap into the Atlantic Ocean.

Nowhere in the mainstream media did anyone draw the connection between that explosion and the fears of rocket scientists concerned about Cassini less than a year earlier.

The payload on the kablooey rocket—apparently a National Reconnaissance Office eavesdropping satellite code-named Vortex—was considered Way Booga Booga Top Secret, but fortunately, there's no indication there was plutonium fuel in the payload.

This time.

And this isn't the first time we came one launch away from a possible major plutonium incident.

Remember the Challenger accident? Challenger's very next scheduled flight would have carried over twenty-five pounds of plutonium. If the shoddy O-rings had held for just one more flight, chances are probably way better than 1 in 100,000 that at least a chunk of coastal Florida would be hot today from more than just the sun.

Oh—and here's the best part: the plutonium isn't even all that necessary. It's not part of the proplusion system; the Pu-238 RTGs are just a hifalutin battery to provide all of 675 big watts to Cassini's instruments. That's relatively gerbil-wheel stuff—just about enough power to crank the handful of replacement light bulbs you keep under the kitchen sink.

You'd think there'd be a safer replacement, and you'd be right. The European Space Agency has already developed solar power cells advanced enough that even a Caltech study by scientists under contract to NASA itself admitted that solar power could get the job done.

And anyway, even if the solar cells aren't quite online, what's the rush? Why now? Is Saturn going someplace?

No, but NASA's money might be. A re-design of Cassini and the RTGs would take years, and given a delay that long caused by an admission of irresponsibility this grave, NASA's cashflow might decay faster than the crap they leave on the ocean floor. Another dozen or so RTG missions are already being scheduled for the near future.

Fun fact: John Pike, director of space policy for the Federation of American Scientists, estimated that the Titan IV is at most only ninety-five percent reliable. Which means the chance of an accident sometime during those dozen launches climbs to roughly one in two.

You wanna flip that coin? Heads, Mr. Wizard learns keen stuff about the rings of Saturn. Tails, Cocoa Beach gets fifty thousand chest X-rays.

Not a real hard risk/reward analysis, is it?

Finally, even though the Cassini probe was launched successfully, consider this: NASA openly admits knowingly risking the lives of innocent people.

In normal human conduct, that's a crime. If you or I drive recklessly near a police cruiser, we get to sit in a squad car whether or not we cause anyone else harm. Fire a gun in the air at a football game, and you face a judge no matter where the bullet lands. When the willful endangerment of others reaches lethal proportions, our system calls that a felony, whether anyone is actually injured or not.

So what do we call NASA's launch of plutonium?

How long will we allow it to continue?

Do we *really* want to wait around for an accident before deciding on the answer?

Part VI

___

Crime & Punishment

Chapter Sixteen

Drug Policy
Locking the Doors
to Perception

I confess: I write these commentaries with chemical assistance. But first, this obligatory public service announcement:

Kids—Say No To Drugs.*

Clear?

And we wonder why our kids don't pay attention to eggs and frying pans.

Anyhow.

I'm not complaining, but churning out the 3500 or so words that comprise a week's worth of these little tirades for the radio, plus a separate lead story for the print edition, takes something like

---

*Except for Ritalin, of course, and maybe Prozac for your folks. For a while Phen-Fen was very good, but now it's very bad, and beer is pretty bad but it's OK in a bar but not on the street, and cigarettes are really bad but they're OK on the street but not in a bar. Marijuana is very very bad, unless you're old enough to have done it a long time ago when it was perfectly fine, but only if you were young at the time. And heroin and cocaine are extremely bad, unless you're helping the CIA in Afghanistan, in which case they're perfectly OK right up until you start bombing our embassies, in which case we start bombing other people who have tenuous connections to you we can't even prove just to make a political point to somebody else, destroying a legitimate pharmaceutical plant whose medicine was the only hope for survival for tens of thousands of famine-stricken Sudanese, which would normally be called terrorism but since *we're* doing it it's called defending democracy.

twelve hours a week. Which isn't exactly coal mining, although the air in L.A. makes it a close call.

(The rest of my week is usually spent: a) taking meetings with Hollywood people who think Noam Chomsky was MacCauley Culkin's co-star in My Girl; b) traveling to college towns less populous than my apartment building, where after a two-hour talk on the history of the Civil Rights movement, all anyone can ask me about is whether Alex Trebek is a nice guy and if he and Ruta Lee ever did it on the High Rollers dice table; and c) tending to a personal life whose plotlines are only vaguely more logical than professional wrestling. Trust me· never get involved with a woman whose bedposts have turnbuckles. But that's what I get for living literally next to the actual Melrose Place.)

I prefer to spend these twelve hours at the keyboard in one long sitting because it makes my brain all fizzy. And for extra zippy bubbles, I often dose myself blind with Downsized America's survival drug of choice: caffeine, now carefully titrated in franchised cafés suddenly showing up on more neighborhood street corners than George Michael.

For our bodies, high doses of caffeine can give us excess stomach acid, nervousness and insomnia, rapid and arrhythmic heartbeats, elevated breathing rates, increased blood sugar and cholesterol levels, overproduction of fibrous tissue and cyst fluid, altered insulin response leading to weight gain and associated health problems, osteoporosis, ulcers, urinary urgency, and even seizures.

For our bosses, however, caffeine can give us a short-term energy boost, a way for the overworked to squeeze an extra hour of productivity out of their exhausted minds.

No wonder it's legal.

And for years I have used caffeine—in daily doses often three times the maximum amount most doctors would consider sane—with my eyes open.

Boy, are my eyes open.

Until today. I'm swearing off caffeine for good.

Right now. Right this minute. Swearing off caffeine. Right now. Now. Swearing it off.

TWITCH

OK.

That all said, let's talk Mark McGwire.

At the 1998 All-Star break, I predicted that none of the major league batting records would be broken. That was before everyone found out that Mark McGwire's post-workout snack includes two-thirds of the Periodic Table.

This guy got big faster than Monica Lewinsky. And it turns out he's boosting his testosterone with a mixture of creatine and some not-quite-steroid thing I can't pronounce and God knows what other biochemical tweaking.

The guy was always a power hitter, but suddenly he's the size of a condo, and now when he plays in Wrigley Field, they don't worry he's gonna break a window across the street, they're afraid he's gonna break the blimp.

And so Roger Maris' home run record suddenly looked easier to obtain than a hall pass from Betty Currie, and some people are still screaming it's not fair, just because McGwire has sprouted a pair of bolts in his neck.

Yeah, well, Roger Maris and Babe Ruth played in Yankee Stadium, where until the 1970s right field was about eleven feet behind second base. You can argue all you want about who's a better hitter. That's the whole *point* of pro sports, which exist mostly so guys in bars can scream at each other through beer spittle and feel like they have a clue while their arteries harden and their jobs are being offloaded to Malaysia.

Get a grip.

Yes, Mark McGwire is a chemically-altered freakboy who corks his bloodstream instead of his bat.

And who *isn't* these days?

How many of the very sportswriters who are so upset because McGwire eats an amino acid regularly adjust their own body chemistry with caffeine, cigarettes, sedatives, anti-depressants, and alcohol?

All of those are legal. So is everything McGwire consumes.

Our entire society is built on better living through chemistry. We'll all suffer the side effects later.

In the meantime, the man hasn't done anything wrong other than excel in an era where scientists gleefully grow babies in test tubes, transplant baboon hearts into people, and grow human ears on the ass of a rat.

Seventy home runs? We're lucky we're still counting in Base 10.

And the only real surprise about McGwire is that he hasn't been cloned.

Yet.

Frying pans still aren't the only unconvincing anti-drug utensils.

When the civic-minded school officials of Ticonderoga, New York, where a pencil manufacturer is a big part of the local economy, decided to tell the kids that drugs are bad, they ordered up a gazillion pencils carrying the slogan:

Too Cool To Do Drugs.

As if kids are gonna be influenced by peer pressure exerted by their writing implements.

As *In These Times* reported, the kids quickly discovered that the pencils carried more messages than anybody intended.

Run "Too Cool To Do Drugs" through a pencil sharpener once or twice, and what do you get?

Cool To Do Drugs.

Oops. Pretty soon, every fourth-grader in the city is giggling and writing with a little nib that says only:

Do Drugs.

So officials ordered a recall. But I think we can cut them some slack. After all, sobriety, or lack thereof, is usually a choice.

Stupidity isn't.

Meanwhile, back in the real world, voters in seven states have approved the use of marijuana for medical reasons.

And good reasons there are. By reducing intraocular pressure, marijuana wails on glaucoma, and since it creates major munchies (say...y'know, Clinton jogged every day for years and still never lost much weight...hmm...) it's also useful in treating life-threatening anorexia, chemotherapy-induced nausea, and the wasting syndrome of many AIDS patients.

Can marijuana really be a medicine? Yup. It was first used as a pain reliever in China over 5000 years ago, and herbalists in India have prescribed it for headaches, insomnia, and nausea for at least 3000 years. Its use in Europe extends all the way back to Galen and the ancient Greeks, although it wasn't widespread until after Napoleon's troops returned from Egypt.

Between 1839 and 1940, cannabis was one of the most common pain relievers in America. Over 100 medical journal articles recommended cannabis for various conditions, and the drug was sold over-the-counter by Parke-Davis, Eli Lilly, and Squibb. Only legislation subsequent to the Marijuana Tax Act of 1937, which had less to do with public health than protecting the paper and synthetic textile markets from automated hemp production, curtailed marijuana's legal medical use in the United States.

However, continuing clinical studies reported that marijuana can even be used as a powerful antidepressant, anticonvulsive, and antibiotic. Illicit medical use remained widespread. Eventually, from 1976 to 1990, the U.S. government supplied over 160,000 marijuana cigarettes to about fifty glaucoma and cancer patients under the Compassionate Investigative New Drug Program. The results were tremendously encouraging, and in 1988, even the DEA's own administrative law judge wrote that "marijuana, in its natural form, is one of the safest therapeutically active substances known."

So there you are.

But never mind all that. Attorney General Janet Reno—whose permanent Mr. Yuk Face frown makes me think she once gargled with Drano and Crazy Glue—flouted democracy, announcing that doctors who prescribe marijuana will still face federal prosecution.

Even though truly dangerous crap like cocaine and morphine are perfectly legal to prescribe, Janet Reno says medical marijuana sends an incorrect message about drugs.

Messages? Hello?!?! For years, Joe Camel was the most recognizable cartoon in America, and—watch carefully—a single televised pro football game contains nearly 100 ads for alcohol.

You want to save kids from drugs? Publicly denounce Jesse Helms and Dick Gephardt as front men for Philip Morris and Anheuser Busch. Interrogate the Commerce Department about subsidizing tobacco sales to third-world children. Arrest any member of the Dallas Cowboys on sight.

Janet Reno should grill noted stoners Bill Clinton, Newt Gingrich, Al Gore, and Rush Limbaugh before screwing with the 60 *million* other Americans who have tried pot—or the doctors who want to use it to save dying people.

Banning medical marijuana doesn't send a message to children; it just criminalizes sick people and the folks who are trying to help them.

In marijuana's place, the government has approved Marinol—Tetrahydrocannabinol (THC), marijuana's go juice, in pure form—from which the drug industry can make a jillion dollars.

Trouble is, Marinol is often useless: patients who need THC precisely to *fight* severe nausea often tend to vomit the capsule.

Duh.

Marinol also has scary physical and psychoactive side effects, and an overdose can kill. Window box pot is cheap, euphoric, and impossible to overdose on.

So is medical marijuana just a trojan horse to legalize pot for recreational use? No. It's about saving lives.

Look, I smoked enough hemp in college to rig the U.S.S. Constitution, but I stopped ten years ago. The cancer risk bugged me, I write better straight, and it's nice to actually remember the words to my favorite reggae songs and Firesign Theatre jokes.

However, before my own father died of chemotherapy last year, my family watched him slowly wither as a result of severe nausea.

Here's how useful marijuana is in cases like my father's: no less than *forty-four percent* of cancer specialists in a recent survey admitted to illegally recommending marijuana at least once.

If Dad had wanted to smoke a joint so he could ease his pain and swallow a solid meal, I would have gladly gotten him one.

I bet you would, too.

Chapter Seventeen

Tobacco
Clinton Could Have Done Worse With That Cigar

Meanwhile, a real drug problem:

As you know, about 400,000 Americans keel over from smoking every year, and most smokers get hooked in their teens.

This is a bad thing.

To demonstrate the human impact of a number like that, whenever I do a lecture that touches on the War On Drugs, I always ask the people in the audience to raise their hand if they've ever lost a loved one or a close friend to crack, heroin, amphetamines, or any other illegal substance.

On average, there are about 200 people in the audience. And not once have more than one or two raised their hands. On most nights not a single hand goes up.

Then I ask everyone to raise their hands if they've ever lost a loved one or a close friend to the effects of cigarette smoking. Every single time, at least half of the hands in the room are raised. Sometimes almost every hand goes up.

When I speak at a college, these people are only twenty years old.

Many college students have already been smoking for more than five years.

And even if they quit, the losses in their lives still mount.

Like you and me, these young people remain fated to spend the rest of their lives watching people they care about die periodically from cigarette and cigar smoking.

Let that sink in for a minute.

It's enough to bring tears on some nights.

And it tells you everything you need to know about America's real drug problem.

What about cigars? Surely they're not the same kind of danger, right? After all, you only smoke one a day, tops, and most cigar smokers don't even inhale the smoke into their lungs. They sell cigars in fancy shops and wine stores. They can't be that bad, can they?

Wrong-o, carcinoma breath. According to the California Department of Health Services, one cigar can pack the punch of up to seventy cigarettes. Another recent study concludes that if you're a cigar smoker, boom—you double your risk of dying of cancer or heart disease. And a third study says that as the wrapper gets moist in your mouth, it passes along the same jolt to your tissues as a good dollop of chewing tobacco.

At this rate, they're gonna figure out that just *looking* at cigars gives you eye cancer.

And thanks to advertising campaigns featuring Hollywood stars and glamorous supermodels, cigar use among young Americans has tripled in recent years.

You want irony? According to the *Washington Post*, the Pentagon has concluded that Cuba now poses essentially zero military threat.

Which means Cuban cigars will harm more Americans in the next seven days than the Cuban military will in the next seven years.

You really want to fight the Cuban menace? Slap Arnold Schwarzeneggar.

You already know that tobacco addiction can lead to heart disease, lung cancer, emphysema, and eye-watering B.O. Now you can add the following to that list: impotence, juvenile delinquency, and genital warts.

That's what I call bang for the buck.

As you already know if you've seen the public service TV ads currently running in California, smoking has been linked to circulation problems which in turn can lead to a severe case of Lo Main Noodle.

Apparenly there's a reason that the cigarettes always come out *after* a game of Race To The Headboard and not before. Maybe handing out cigars when a child is born isn't a celebration, but a form of tribal birth control.

Gee, if only Clinton had smoked *his* cigars…

Meanwhile, a new study in the *Archives of General Psychiatry* suggests that pregnant women who smoke more than ten cigarettes a day *quadruple* their chance of giving birth to a juvenile delinquent.

In other words, sleep with Joe Camel, give birth to Beavis and Butthead.

Expectant mothers should think about the consequences. Sure, a few precious little puffs might seem relaxing right now. But ten or twelve years later, think of the stress when your kid starts lying, stealing, setting fires, and torturing animals.

If you smoke while you're pregnant, someday you won't need a cigarette; you'll need a Prozac and a taser gun.

And finally, a new study out of Australia indicates a side effect of smoking guaranteed to get the attention of any teenager on Earth:

Genital warts.

See, it even got *your* attention.

The acute, yicky phase of a common genital wart infection, which often lasts just a couple of weeks for a non-smoker, can last for smokers anywhere from an extra 6 months to 3 *years*.

In which case, the study also notes, your sex life basically disappears.

No wonder the Marlboro Man spends so much time alone with his horse.

So what can we do about cigarettes? Improving the warnings might help, but don't hold your breath. Unless you're stuck in an elevator with a tobacco addict.

You've seen those little rectangles on the sides of American cigarette packages, warning of all of the above disorders, plus stroke, high blood pressure, gout, warts, scrapie, rickets, Dutch Elm Disease, and taco neck.

Unfortunately, no matter what warnings they write on the sides of the packages, we get used to the little square, and so we never read it.

The next round of tobacco warnings could contain the source code for Windows, the recipe for Coca-Cola, and Sarah Michelle Gellar's home phone number. Nobody would notice.

But that won't stop Canada from trying. Their Health Minister wants to make sixty percent of the whole package a warning about diseases and poisons and how smoking can even hamper your sex life. Which we know anyway. Ever french kissed someone with a cigarette in their mouth? Bleugh.

Maybe warnings can work. But Canada's still not taking them far enough. You want to scare smokers? Put a dark-spotted chest X-ray on sixty percent of the package. Put a picture of an Iron Lung and a summary of the associated medical bills on the sides. And on the front, put a mirror, because nobody thinks it can happen to them.

Sounds radical, I know. But it's just truth in advertising.

Another public health measure that would help: clean up campaign financing in Washington. Last year, Congress was finally considering—and an American president was actually supporting—a comprehensive bill aimed at lowering that grisly toll through a variety of means: public education and anti-smoking programs, gradually raising the cigarette taxes over several years, allowing the FDA to regulate tobacco, and so on.

Amid widespread popular support, the bill breezed through the Senate Commerce Committee by a vote of 19-1. A similar bill was pending in the House. Passage and signature into law seemed imminent. Health officials were thrilled.

Tobacco companies weren't.

OK, so if you're a tobacco guy, what's the best spin you can come up with? Simple: Latch onto the tax part and harp on it, as if the whole shebang was really nothing more than a sneaky ploy to raise taxes.

And that's why for several months you saw a bunch of TV ads, where people on the street say stuff like "I'll vote against anybody who'd raise tobacco taxes," and then at the end you might have noticed it was paid for by cigarette companies.

This sort of message is called an Issue Ad, and it's perfectly legal…as long as it's not part of a backroom deal to benefit a specific candidate or candidates.

However…

It turns out that just before the tobacco bill was scheduled to come to a vote, Senator Mitch McConnell—a Kentucky Republican whose #1 source of PAC money has been the tobacco industry—reportedly told other Republicans that the tobacco guys had promised to continue running the ads all the way to November.

The ads would therefore assist the fall campaigns of anybody voting to kill the bill.

And the tobacco bill collapsed shortly thereafter.

If indeed, as it appears, a deal existed—and ads were exchanged for votes—this is a clear case of widespread bribery, a blatant criminal violation of federal election laws. And so the criminal division of the Justice Department began asking questions.

McConnell and the smokelords insist there was no deal—but sure enough, the TV ads continued to run for months after the bill was killed.

In fact, the tobacco dudes actually budgeted over $100 million to keep buying ads all the way to November—focusing almost entirely in states where (guess what!) Republicans who helped kill the tobacco bill were in tight races.

In Missouri, Nevada, and Georgia, where GOP Senators who voted to kill the tobacco bill were considered especially vulnerable, the ads ran over a *thousand times*.

The story appeared in the *Baltimore Sun*, but most other newspapers never even mentioned the investigation, contenting themselves with the latest revelations about Monica Lewinsky's ability to suppress reverse peristalsis.

But what Monica did for Bill in private, the Justice Department came to suspect the tobacco lobby did for several dozen members of the U.S. Senate, to the tune of a *hundred million dollars*—affecting, in turn, billions in the federal budget, the health of the entire nation, and indeed the very democratic process itself.

Tell me what's the bigger scandal.

According to reports on the latest election cycle from the Federal Election Commission, the tobacco industry poured money into both the Republican and Democratic parties at about *five times* the pace of the corresponding period four years ago. Eighty percent of the dough went to the GOP majority.

You can pretend that maybe all the tobacco money flooding the wallets of Congress wasn't intended to influence anybody's vote. But if not, then why exactly *did* the tobacco guys suddenly start pouring millions of dollars into campaign coffers? After agreeing to fork over over a third of a trillion dollars, they suddenly all feel some extra cash burning holes in their pockets?

An R.J. Reynolds spokesperson told the AP that it wasn't *their* fault—the politicians are to blame, suddenly pressuring the tobacco boys to fork over like never before. Oh, really? Not to defend a politician—Johnnie Cochran might have trouble with that feat— but it's not like the Congressmen are the ones whose empires might depend on the liability deal.

And here's the lowdown on the tobacco deal itself:

Yeah, the bad guys have to pour out hundreds of billions of dollars, and they give up billboards, vending machines, Joe Camel, and the Marlboro Man. Cigarette packs will now have scarier warning labels, smoking will be banned from many public places, and manufacturers will fund teen anti-smoking programs.

The headlines sound great, right? Read the fine print.

- Annual tobacco-associated health costs are about $100 billion, but the companies will only be paying about $15 billion a year. We're settling for fifteen cents on the dollar.

- In exchange for the payout, class action suits will be abolished, and individuals will be forbidden from seeking punitive damages. (That's arguably a violation of the Seventh Amendment guarantee of due process, but nobody cares.)

- The tobacco companies won't pay the settlement; consumers will. The cost of cigarettes will simply rise to cover the expense. They'll lose a few smokers, but the loss will be covered by decreased marketing expenses as a result of the new restrictions. End of story.

- Philip Morris, RJR, and the rest are sprawling multinationals with major cash flow outside of cigarettes. Some stock brokers consider RJR's Nabisco Foods division alone worth more than the parent corporation's total market capitalization. By removing most potential liability suits from the equation, several tobacco analysts projected Philip Morris and RJR stocks to rise, possibly as high as thirty percent in the next year. On Wall Street, crime pays.

- All five of the majors already make most of their tobacco money overseas, so they'll just accelerate their marketing into developing countries. By protecting the tobacco industry's profits here, the deal guarantees millions of future tobacco deaths in the Third World.

This was pretty much the deal pending before Newt Gingrich's House of Representatives at the same time Newt needed to come up with $300,000 to cover his ethics fine. And a leading tobacco lobbying firm hired Bob Dole, giving him an unusual $300,000 signing bonus. And six days later Dole "loaned" Newt $300,000.

And so the deal reached the floor of a Congress controlled by a GOP whose two leading financial contributors were tobacco companies.

And idiots in the media actually wonder why working-class Americans feel like their vote no longer matters...

However, as you recall, in the first breath of fresh air a tobacco company has ever provided, Liggett finally admitted that "cigarette smoking causes...lung cancer, heart and vascular disease, and emphysema."

Let's not stop there.

Maybe someday Liggett will also concede that the only reason they confessed was for the money—limiting their own liability via settlement, thereby making themselves more attractive as a takeover candidate.

Maybe Philip Morris will also admit that they engaged, in the words of a Minnesota state court judge, in "an egregious attempt to hide" incriminating information about their manufacturing and marketing practices.

Maybe R.J. Reynolds will acknowledge that, as newly-released documents reveal, in 1984 they made a "long-term commitment... to younger adult smoker programs." Following this decision, the Joe Camel ads were produced, and the number of children addicted to RJR's death sticks increased by a factor of *fifty*.

Maybe the ad agencies and PR flacks who whitewash tobacco will begin creating new campaigns to alert the public that cigarettes are America's *real* drug problem. Maybe they'll invent cuddly cartoon characters—Mighty Coughin' Power Rangers, Nicotine Patch Kids, Tracheoto-Me-Elmo—to teach our kids that more than *forty times* as many of our loved ones die from cigarettes as all illegal drugs *combined*.

Maybe they'll admit pouring money into "Smoker's Rights" front groups whose only real purpose is to keep as many people addicted as possible. Maybe they'll also admit how dopey their arguments are. (Suppose I enjoy wearing a dime bag of plutonium strapped to my left thigh; does that give me the "right" to irradiate everyone around me? Spitting on a sidewalk can be restricted, but blowing carcinogens into the air an infant is breathing is a "right?" Start the car, honey, there's a sale down at Grip Mart. Let's go get us a Family Pack.)

Maybe they'll concede funding think-tank White Papers pushing liability-judgment limits as "Tort Reform." And maybe the

Newts and Jesses turning these policies into law will admit to accepting massive tobacco contributions.

Maybe the Republican Party will confess that its leading contributor is Philip Morris, and four of its top ten supporters are tobacco companies. Maybe Bob Dole will admit that his insane comments questioning smoking's addictive power were colored by his love for Marlboro money and frequent flights on U.S. Tobacco company jets.

Maybe Al Gore will cop to his obscene lie at the 1996 Democratic convention, when he grandstanded his sister's smoking-related death as an anti-tobacco epiphany. Maybe he'll admit to soliciting cigarette money for years after her death, once proudly boasting to a convention of tobacco growers of his love for harvesting and rolling tobacco by hand.

Maybe the shareholders who profit from tobacco companies will realize their moral (if not legal) liability for the cancer trade.

Maybe the Partnership for a Drug Free America, creators of "This Is Your Brain" and other ads—useless in stopping drug abuse, but great for maintaining phony Drug War hysteria—will admit that much of their funding originates with tobacco companies.

Maybe *Time* and *Newsweek* will concede the remote possibility that their own drug-like dependence on tobacco ads just might have influenced their coverage of America's tobacco holocaust for over forty years.

Maybe public figures who glamorize smoking—Letterman, Limbaugh, Madonna, etc.—will admit they're encouraging children to become addicted. Maybe they'll learn from Humphrey Bogart, Steve McQueen, Groucho Marx, Arthur "Smoke 'Em By The Carton" Godfrey, Edward R. Murrow, and several of the Marlboro Men in the ads themselves, all of whom died of lung cancer.

Maybe storeowners who sell cigarettes will realize you're as much to blame as the manufacturers. R.J. Reynolds needs you as badly as the Medellin Cartel needed Freeway Ricky Ross. Maybe you'll stop selling products that kill your customers.

And maybe you smokers reading this right now will admit that you're—putting it mildly—drug-addicted fools. Maybe you'll get help to stop selfishly endangering others and cutting your own life short.

Or maybe that's too much to ask.

Chapter Eighteen

Sentencing

Steal This Book—
And Get Life Without Parole

For once, the good news: the Justice Department says the violent crime rate is at its lowest level since they started the index.

They're really only talking 1997 data, since the FBI takes longer to transfer files than AOL. But the latest number is just thirty-nine violent crimes per thousand people. When the survey started in the 1970s, the number was twenty-five percent higher, and it went up drastically in the '80s before dropping in the 1990s.

Experts say it's the economy or changing demographics. The truth is, since correlation does not equal causation, nobody really knows for sure. Ice cream sales and the murder rate both peak in July; that doesn't mean one causes the other, unless we're willing to accept brainfreeze as a form of temporary insanity.

Which means you can also argue that the changing crime rate is connected to the band Journey, whose record sales track the national crime rate almost perfectly.

But the bad news is this: according to polls, people's perception is that violent crime is still increasing. Two-thirds of Americans think the crime rate is still going up, and only one percent of us fully realize how fast the streets are getting safer.

Op-ed writers have theories about all this: violence on TV, sensational news reporting, and so on.

Maybe there's another reason.

No, Journey hasn't had a hit in years, but that doesn't mean that there aren't singers just as godawful out there, driving ordinary people to the brink of senseless violence.

Michael Bolton, people.

Figure 23a

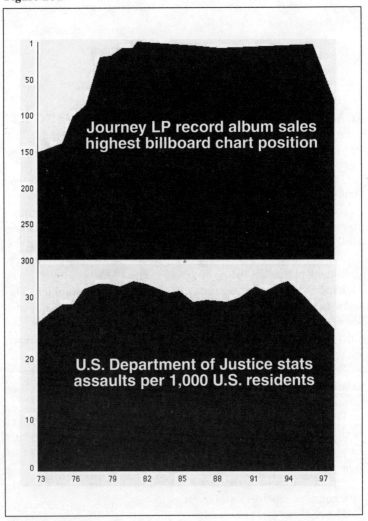

Correlation does not equal causation

Either that, or lead singer Steve Perry should be put away for good.

The menace that is Bryan Adams.

Cher.

Perhaps *these* are the modern faces of crime in America.

Only when these dark forces are stopped will peace truly have come to our land.

Actually, bad rock and roll isn't the only menace loose in our society. The other major menace is: our society.

According to the latest figures from the Centers for Disease Control, United States citizens are #1 among residents of all developed countries in shooting each other dead.

All together now: *U-S-A! U-S-A!*

Bring it on, Canada; we'll kick your national-health-care-receiving ass!

And by the way, the numbers are per capita, so we didn't win on size. Just pure lunatic violence.

You're almost three hundred times more likely to shoot somebody here than if you live in Japan. Of course, in Japan, you're about three thousand times more likely to make a living by knocking people down with your enormous stomach. So we still don't have a monopoly on weirdness.

Here's a perfect example of why we're Tops of the Pops: the state of Kentucky has made it legal for ministers to carry concealed handguns while delivering sermons.

Apparently there was a string of people pulling out shotguns at the end of services and walking off with the collection plates. Somebody's taking the words "praise the Lord and pass the ammunition" a little too seriously.

So the Kentucky legislature voted 76-9 to let the God guys pack heat.

Excuse me, but somehow I can't see Jesus—avatar of forgiveness, messenger of peace, grand bestower of slack—giving the Sermon On The Mount with a TEC-9 strapped to his hip. Maybe I missed something.

I guess for some people, turning the other cheek is just a way of buying time to reload.

Here's another kind of street crime to consider, one with constitutional implications nobody seems to realize:

The city of Los Angeles has banned the use of leaf blowers. Personally, I'm OK with that. Leaf blowers are too loud and they stink. Kind of like the movie *Armageddon* in backpack form.

And L.A. is just the largest and latest of hundreds of cities and townships which have banned leaf blowers in recent years.

Ironically, however, it's a good thing leaf blowers are only a horrid nuisance. If they could actually be used to kill someone, then we probably *couldn't* ban them.

Think about it—if you could put a leaf blower on a turbo-thrust setting and blast someone's head clean off, the NRA would claim that leaf blowers are constitutionally protected.

But the worst you can do to somebody with a leaf blower (so far, anyhow) is bop them in the shins or give them lung cancer, so it's below the NRA's radar. "Annoying" they don't bother with; "deadly" goes right in the Rolodex.

Which means if leaf blower manufacturers want to keep their product on the market, maybe the best thing they can do is create a screw-on nozzle that turns an ordinary leaf blower into a gasoline-powered blowgun of death.

Next thing you know, Charlton Heston will start marching arm-in-arm with poor laborers, bellowing in his best Moses voice:

"Let my people blow!"

It wouldn't be the first time a right-winger took a surprising stance on a political issue. Remember, Pat Robertson once opposed the death penalty.

You remember Karla Faye Tucker, the foxy-looking Bible-thumping artery-slashing double-murder babe who wanted clemency because she found God and stuff, which meant now she could help her fellow out-of-control axe murderers get a grip on things. Besides axe handles.

Karla Faye was on *20/20*, *Larry King Live*, and a bunch of other TV shows. Why? Not because she might be innocent. Nope. She confessed. And it's not because many folks down there are re-think-

ing capital punishment. She's in Texas, remember, where they executed more people last year than all other states combined, possibly because the Cowboys had a lousy season. People need something to do.

But what *everyone* knew was this: the only reason anyone gave a ding-dang about this woman was because she was a babe, which gives the TV cameras something to point at. Don't kid yourself. What if she looked like Shaquille O'Neal in drag? Or suppose she converted—not to Christianity, but to Islam? Either way, then we're not having this conversation.

But given this dewy-eyed, full-lipped, tawny-haired, Deuteronomy-reciting pin-up-looking chick, suddenly even Pat Robertson was willing to forgive the small matter of those two handcrafted veinrippings.

No human soul is more or less redeemable because of the container it came in. This ain't pleasant to admit, but in our prisons, people often live or die depending on the color of their skin.

Justice is supposed to be blind. If it ain't, it ain't justice.

There are people on Death Row right this minute for whom redemption isn't even the question, because evidence of their actual innocence exists.

Oppose the death penalty for Karla Faye Tucker, and morally, you have to oppose the death penalty, period.

That's one of the reasons why the American Bar Association voted overwhelmingly for a moratorium on executions until the death penalty can be administered with fairness, due process, and minimum risk that innocent people will die.

That day will never come.

There are 3100 people on Death Row. Virtually all are poor. Most are minorities. Many are mentally ill or minors. Some are innocent.

Azikiwe Kambule is a seventeen-year-old South African boy, convicted of a murder in which he was essentially a bystander. He had no criminal record or history of violence and cooperated completely with the police. Mississippi intends to execute him.

The only other countries that execute minors are Bangladesh, Iran, Iraq, Pakistan, Rwanda, Saudi Arabia, and Yemen. The U.S. executes more minors than all other nations combined.

Madison Hobley is a Bible student who worked providing medical equipment to the elderly. He lost his wife and son when an arsonist burned their apartment building. Arrested without evidence by the notorious Area Two Violent Crimes Unit of the Chicago Police—whose commander has since been fired for torturing more than forty blacks—Hobley was beaten, partially suffocated, and threatened at gunpoint. At trial, Area Two cops claimed that Hobley eventually signed a confession, but they—get this—*threw it away* after it became wet in the rain. Hobley was convicted. Illinois intends to execute him.

Per capita, the six governments which lead the world in executing their own people are China, Iran, Iraq, Nigeria, Florida, and Texas.

These are not isolated incidents. The UN Commission on Human Rights recently noted that Maurice Andrews, Robert Brecheen, Willie Clisby, Anthony Joe Larette, Mario Marquez, and Luis Mata were all on Death Row in spite of mental incapacity. The UN also noted that Larry Griffin, Nicholas Ingraham, Jesse Jacobs, Gregory Resnover, and Dennis Waldon Stockton were very likely innocent.

All eleven have now been executed.

If you must kill someone, be white. Being black quadruples your risk of a death sentence. And if you must kill someone, you'll have an easier time of it if you kill a black person. Kill a white, and you're twice as likely to be executed.

The Fourteenth Amendment guarantees equal protection and due process for all. The death penalty is a sick joke on the Constitution.

There is *no* credible evidence that executions deter crime. Causation still isn't clear, but crime correlates far better to population density, wealth inequity, and the concentration of young males than to any law enforcement factors.

Capital punishment also costs two or three times more than life without parole. Few defendants plead guilty to a capital charge, so most every death penalty trial becomes a jury trial. We're wasting tens of millions of dollars.

Secure prisons already exist: in California, not one prisoner sentenced to life without parole has been released since the option was created in 1977.

Allowed to live, inmates can be put to work, with the proceeds benefitting the victims' families. Given this sentencing option, seventy percent of Americans prefer it.

Besides, if the accused is later exonerated, the jail door can open. You can't raise the dead.

After sixteen years on death row, Anthony Porter, forty-three, walked out of the Cook County Jail in February 1999 after a local journalism professor and his class proved he was wrongly convicted of two 1982 murders. Porter, who has an IQ of fifty-one, came within two days of execution by lethal injection before the Illinois Supreme Court decided that his case required another look. Since then, a key witness has recanted his testimony, saying police had pressured him, and another man finally confessed on videotape that he had killed the two victims.

The Eighth Amendment prohibits cruel and unusual punishment. Ever witness an execution? They're *plenty* cruel and unusual. Hangings often slowly strangle the victim, who can remain conscious for much of the process. Electrocutions can take up to ten minutes, as can the gas chamber. Some lethal injections have taken more than twenty minutes. (And yes, they really *do* swab your arm with alcohol first, just so you don't die with an infection.)

Florida's electric chair is nicknamed "Old Sparky" because it sometimes causes the heads of its victims to burst into flames. Local judges refuse to consider this cruel or unusual. Apparently, flaming heads are a common site in Florida. You see them at spring training baseball games all the time. That's how Florida fans cheer. Home run! High five! *Woooof!*

Florida state officials even brag about the practice as a means of demonstrating their toughness on crime. Which means cruelty is entirely the point.

No other western industrialized nation does this to its own people.

Your habeus corpus rights are supposed to be your federal guarantee that local officials respect the Constitution. If a state court jails you wrongly, you have—*had*, sorry—the right to appeal the legality of your conviction in federal court.

How often is this necessary? State judges are often elected, which means justice becomes secondary to looking studly for the voters. In the last twenty years, nearly *half* of the state court decisions in capital cases have been overturned.

Willingness to kill is not equivalent to moral strength.

In a similar display, in 1996 Congress passed, the President signed, and the Supreme Court upheld the "Antiterrorism and Death Penalty Act," which imposed an unprecedented one-year time limit on habeus corpus appeals.

So what happens if your proof of innocence emerges after the first year has passed? Simple: you die.

In *Leonel Herrera v. Collins*, the Court has held that the Consitution does not protect state prisoners from execution, *even given new evidence of innocence*. Chief Justice Rehnquist actually wrote that "entertaining claims of actual innocence" would have a "disruptive effect...on the need for finality."

In other words, your actual guilt or innocence just doesn't matter that much.

Leonel Herrera, who was probably innocent, was executed shortly thereafter.

Capital punishment is quickly transforming the Bill of Rights itself into a Dead Man Walking.

The ABA has taken an important step in acknowledging that the death penalty doesn't work.

The next step is to accept that it never will.

Index

About the Author

Bob Harris is a syndicated radio humorist whose daily commentaries air on about 100 stations nationwide, winning 1997 awards from both the Associated Press and L.A. Press Club. He's also a leading guest speaker on college campuses, bringing talks on subjects from campaign financing to the civil rights movement to almost 300 universities. A columnist for *Mother Jones* magazine's online edition, Bob's also a successful stand-up comedian and five-time champion on TV's *Jeopardy!*, which is what makes Mom proudest. Bob lives in Hollywood, where he works sweatshop hours and swears off dating actresses on a regular basis. He can be reached through his website, www.bobharris.com.